I've Lived It, I've Loved It!

An anecdotal memoir
by

Mel Corren

UPDATED
2016

BOOK AND COVER DESIGN BY
DONALD CORREN

COVER PHOTO BY ZENOGRAPHER
GLENN WILLIAMS

Lovingly dedicated to those past and present who've contributed to the title of this memoir, and especially to my forebears, who blessed me with the opportunity to be an American.

TABLE OF CONTENTS

The Right Place, The Right Time

"Life is a dream."

This phrase, oft-repeated by my grandmother, has become even more salient to me in my waning years.

In a roundabout way, it was she who started me on the road to writing the following pages. She taught me how to go about living in the world, the value of the moment, and a love for the family and its history complete with warts and beauty marks.

It was her love of family photos, which hung on every wall of her home (and now on mine), that started me on the path of collecting and digitizing those I inherited from her, along with those I collected on my own.

When I retired from my workaday life, I decided to write this book for two reasons. First, I realized that if the history of the family was to be written, it would be up to me – the oldest link between the generation of immigrants and those of us born here.

Second, in reliving my life through my memories, I have come to realize just how lucky I am to have been born at the time I was, in the family I was, and most of all in the United States of America. All of these conditions contributed to making my life different and better than the great majority of those who are born every day.

I'm also aware of the sheer luck which separated me from the masses of my Jewish kin who were so brutally annihilated by the Nazis and their assistants, making me appreciate even more the hardships my forebears endured so that I could live my life in this land of opportunity.

PHOTO:

The author at an early age (Austin Studios, Stockton, Ca.)

"In the Beginning"

My good fortune began before I was born, when Schiffera Korin, my Grandfather's oldest sister, married Herschel (Kantorowitz) Davidson, who later decided to emigrate to the United States of America. His motivation for leaving his hometown in the Ukraine was twofold. First, he had heard of the opportunities in the western part of that new country, namely California, due to the discovery of gold near Tuleburg – later renamed Stockton – where a cousin of his had already settled. Second, at the end of the 19th century, Russia was increasingly an unsafe place for Jews.

Economic conditions were bad, creating the need for a scapegoat, a role Jews throughout history have unfortunately been called upon to fulfill. Furthermore, as a result of wars on many fronts, the Russian army was doing poorly. It needed more and more cannon fodder, which caused the tsar to conscript increasing numbers of soldiers, even kidnapping young men – Jews among them – to serve in the military. Often a very young boy would be taken from his family and never heard from again. Life was hard in the *shtetls*, where Jews were compelled to live and were governed by a societal structure. The person beneath the regional representative of the Russian government was the chief rabbi – the *shtetls* – and all questions regarding ethics, religion and law (which most often were associated) were decided by the *rebbe* or a group of lesser, appointed learned men.

Then, at the end of the 19th century, a dramatic change occurred in the way of life for young Jewish men, creating both the desire and the opportunity for them to flee the *shtetls* and ultimately Russia itself. The major factor

contributing to this change was a breach in the ranks of Orthodox Judaism, which caused many young Jewish men to begin thinking in more modern and secular ways. This phenomenon, combined with the advent of the Industrial Revolution – which afforded the average person the opportunity to find work in new factories – created a wanderlust which had been dormant in Jewish youth for many years.

So, along with the Russian peasants looking for a better life in the cities, came young Jews wanting to leave the old ways and eager to find jobs in the sweat shops. These jobs offered low wages and poor working conditions, but a far less restrictive life than they were accustomed to in the *shtetls*.

When Grandpa Mendel experienced this newly found freedom from strict religious observance and decided to leave, it was to follow his older sister to the fresh new world, the United States of America.

PHOTOS:

Schiffera and Herschel (Kantorovitz) Davidson
Mendel and friend before leaving Russia
(Photographers unknown)
Manifest of ship bringing Mendel to America

Departure and Arrival

Grandpa Mendel Corren – "Korin" before arriving in the U.S., where, as he often told, an Irishman re-spelled his name – had been a merchant in or near Poltava, a city near Kiev, Ukraine. On August 25, 1901, he bade farewell to his pregnant wife and child, not knowing whether he would ever see them again. He took time to pose with his a cappella group (he was very involved in the arts, singing in the synagogue and performing with this group of singers and actors) one hour before traveling overland to Hamburg, where he embarked on the S.S. Bulgaria.

Grandpa Mendel, his sister and her children arrived in New York Harbor on September 7, 1901. Traveling in steerage with children of all ages must

have been difficult, although, many passengers reported that nevertheless there was much singing and dancing aboard.

According to family lore, Schiffera's young son Sollie, who was then about fourteen, brought the food and tea around to the family in steerage, and Mendel, who was about 23, kept everyone entertained and in stitches. The story goes that he was so handsome and had such a great personality that he had to be constantly reminded by Schiffera that he was a married man.

A disturbing event happened the day before the ship docked in New York Harbor. President McKinley was assassinated. The killer was suspected of being a Russian, which proved to be untrue; however, Grandpa and his fellow passengers, also from Russia, were, for a time, afraid to disembark for fear of reprisals.

Schiffera and her family left the ship and headed by train directly to

Stockton, a well-situated small town located on a river that served as a supply base for the miners who had come in 1849 to hunt for gold in the foothills above Sacramento, some 45 miles north. She later changed her married name to Davidson, the name taken by members of her family who had preceded her. Schiffera's husband, Herschel (Kantorowicz) Davidson, had come earlier to join members of his family in Stockton. These Jewish immigrants, who had been merchants in the old country, joined those who were supplying goods to the miners.

Meanwhile, Mendel detoured circuitously through Duluth, Minnesota, where he visited with his uncle Hilly (Henry on his tombstone, which is in Colma, California). Hilly had spent a few years in England en-route to Duluth, and he and his wife, Dora, had already begun a large family. His family included a daughter, Goldie Carrie Levine, who was born in 1900, a year before Mendel's arrival in America, and was the next to the youngest child in the Levine family of three boys and eight girls. Many years later, this same Goldie would marry Mendel's second son, Samuel (Sam), and be my mother. Mendel then headed west to Stockton, where he rejoined his sister and her

family, ready to begin a new life.

Our immigrant ancestors arrived with no knowledge of the language or customs. Despite these obstacles, they settled in, began learning the language and the ways of their new home, and, with the aid of relatives already here and the Jewish Agency, began making a living.

During the first several years, their main objective was to save for the day they could send for the rest of their families.

PHOTOS:

Grandpa Mendel (seated right, head on hand) with his A Cappella group in Russia. The back of the photo reads, "One hour before leaving for America."
Ellis Island, 2001
(Photographers unknown)

Grandma Noonie

Her given name was Anna

Grandma Noonie was married to Mendel Corren, the son of Moshe (Moses) and Esther Corren. She was the daughter of Leah Metz whose husband died before she came to America in the early years of the 20th century.

Anna had lived with her family in a *shtetl* in the county of Chernigov near Kiev. When her father died, her mother sent her to live with relatives – a custom sometimes practiced by widowed women in the *shtetls*.

Anna was "farmed out" to an uncle who had been a soldier in the tsar's army until retirement. Because of his service, he was allowed to live in one of the larger towns otherwise off limits to Jews.

In contrast to the other Jews in the small schtetls, Grandma Noonie spoke as though she lived in the lap of luxury. She talked of servants – and it might have been that she was somewhat in this category herself, since "farmed out" relatives' children were often pressed into service. The arrangement proved advantageous for her, as her uncle owned a small grocery store and was able to offer her the opportunity to be better educated than most women of her time and station.

We were told that after she returned to the *shtetl* and married Mendel, she longed for the life of the city. Since it was impossible for him to live there, he decided to leave Russia and make a new start for them in America. I believe there were other reasons as well, but this was a romantic story that caught our fancy.

Anna had quite a broad knowledge of the world for her time and place. Her advice was always sage, as well as practical. For instance, years before the talk of sun damage causing cancer, she advocated the wearing of a head covering, not solely for religious reasons – Orthodox Jews always have their heads covered as religious practice – but to protect the body from the rays of the sun. She would lecture anyone who came to her house about the need to be protected from the sun, and whenever I arrived hatless, she would march me over to the little department store nearby to buy me a hat. The shopkeeper, always good-natured, brightened even more when Grandma brought me into his store. I can still hear his melodious Italian accent as he greeted me with "Hello, my boy."

Grandma Noonie was easy to locate on the street, because even in the heat of summer, she would have on a white coat, gloves and a hat to ward off the rays of the sun. She also preached to anyone not wearing a hat and to men not wearing suspenders – partly because the sun was an *imndling* (curse), and partly because a tight belt caused indigestion and G-d knows what else. Also, as she reasoned, if you didn't wear hats and suspenders, how would those who make them feed their families?

Entire books have been written in celebration of the cooking abilities of the *Yiddisha mama* and grandmother, but Grandma Noonie did not fit this pattern, except for some of the idiosyncrasies of her "cuisine".

She was famous with her grandchildren for the "hamlettes" she made anytime of the day, usually served with hot chocolate and dry hard baked toast, or as she called it, "melba toast."

The "hamlette" (sans ham) was in effect, an omelette, made with eggs and evaporated milk, and, as was her specialty, burnt on the bottom. The hot chocolate was powdered cocoa, evaporated milk and sugar. The ratio of water to milk was more than you would ordinarily expect, but it tasted better than any other, anywhere. The slow baked "melba toast" was marvelous for dunking in the chocolate, and the three delicacies together made getting up in the morning at Grandma Noonie's house a pleasure. However – and this was a big however – you couldn't get any one of the three items until after the *Maydeahni*, the Hebrew morning prayer. At night, the *Shmah* preceded the hot chocolate and cookies before going to sleep. There were other delicacies: the *gebrutanz*, the *pitzah*, and a few of the other dishes I can still taste to this day.

Grandma Noonie's *gebrutanz* was a chuck roast that was roasted in a blue/black oval enamel roasting pan with onions, potatoes, carrots, and garlic. The fact is, any meat roasted in this way was termed *gebrutanz*, even fowl. This too was severely burnt and adhered to the bottom of the pan, creating a caramelized crust that was delicious to scrape off and eat, much like licking the bowl when a cake was being baked. But, the person who had to clean the pan was not exactly thrilled with the job it created.

The *pitzah* was a very special Russian dish made with cow hooves, chicken feet, or any other item that created a gelatin texture. (It is made outside of Jewish circles with pig knuckles.) To these basics you add an outrageous amount of garlic, and I can tell you, it needs getting used to.

Grandma Noonie also baked a wonderful *honigliych* (honey cake). She lined the bottom of the cake pan with wax paper, which burnt to the bottom of the cake and to the pan, making it nearly impossible to get it off of either. Anyone who ever tasted it will tell you that it was worth the effort.

Despite all these delicious dishes, I once heard one of my uncles after being berated by his mother for something he did or did not do, respond by asking, "What did I ever get around here besides herring and potatoes?" Which reminds me of the saying I often heard from Grandma when she would bemoan the difficulties of her life: "*I gepumked vasser und genemen arrine borders*" (I pumped water and took in boarders.) I knew she must have pumped water, but I had never heard of her taking in borders, except for an occasional *meshulach* (a holy man soliciting funds).

Another wonderful Noonie-ism: Our older son, Howard, was studying Russian language and Slavic literature at UC Berkeley circa 1970 and had the opportunity to study for a semester in what was then known as Leningrad (now St. Petersburg). He assumed his Russian-born great grandmother, at that time in her early 90s, would be thrilled to hear that news.

He didn't get what he expected. *"Far vos gaist du dorten? Fun dorten habt men gekomen!* (Why are you going there? We came from there!)," Noonie exclaimed. That summed up her feelings about the "old country."

Grandma Noonie remained her vibrant self until she sold her home. Unfortunately, this also included the sale of the old player piano on which we all had such a fine time. Those of us who remember it still lament its loss. She moved to an apartment across the street from the college. There she slowly became an old woman, reminiscent of her own mother, and the many others who had lived to ripe old ages. From this apartment she moved to a duplex on Walnut Street, which was owned by her son Maurice. She lived there with aid from young girls until she could no longer take care of her basic needs, at which time she moved to a newly built convalescent home where she lived out her final days.

An interesting and humorous incident took place at our home on the very evening of the day she moved to this "home." I had picked her up and brought her home for dinner, as we all had done frequently, to make her evenings more enjoyable. Usually, when she came to any of our houses to eat, she would announce at the start of the meal that she had *"cummen up upgegessane"* – that she had already eaten – but when served, she would enjoy the vegetables, salad and dessert with relish, belying that fact. The reason for her announcement was to make the hostess feel comfortable with the fact that she would not eat the entree because she kept Kosher, and would not eat the meat dishes. On this particular night, though, something different happened. As she sat down at the table, she announced, *"Ergirt nisht far mir ahz Ich ess alas yetst. Der doktor und de rabbe haut mir gezuct ahz ich ken alas essen ver ich voint yetzt"* (Don't worry about me, the doctor and the rabbi told me I can eat anything where I'm living now), capping it off in broken English: "I vish I vould have done it lung time ago."

PHOTOS:

Anna Metz Corren
...in Russia
...at our house on Lakeside Drive
...on Main Street, Stockton
(Photographers unknown)

Tzedacha (Charity)

During the Depression, Grandma Noonie had a continuous string of down-and-out men coming from the railroad yards to her house, just a few blocks away. She made "sangwiches,"as she called them, for the *ourima menschen* (the poor people). For her this was both a labor of love and a *tzedacha* (charity). It was almost a full-time job, for which she would recruit her grandchildren whenever we came to the house.

We helped her with the shopping, the writing of notes and the distribution of the "sangwiches." "Sangwiches" were made of anything left over from meals or from a special section in the ice box (no refrigerator), which was kept supplied from the two little grocery stores on each corner: Troglia's on Center Street and DeRicco's on El Dorado Street. We would be sent to buy the white and yellow sliced cheeses and white bread at either of these two grocery stores. Grandma alternated so that they would share equally in her purchases.

The DeRicco's son, Lawrence, who was a little older than me, later became the president of Delta College, the community college in Stockton, which recently named a new building on campus after him and his wife, Alma.

We liked it best when Grandpa gave Grandma the grocery money because when we returned from the store we were told to keep the change, but when she had no money and we were told to put it on the tab, we knew that we, too, were a part of the charity.

Grandma would hold court at her house for the indigents (almost everyone else called them bums, tramps, or hobos in those days), who in reality were down-and-out men who could not find work due to the Depression, and she practiced the biblical edict that you should feed the hungry and clothe the naked without robbing them of their dignity.

These men rode the freight cars in their quest for employment. If they couldn't get into a car, they hung onto the undercarriages of the box cars so as not to be discovered by the railroad guards (hence the term "Riding the rails"). They were for the most part upright men, looking for work in the fields or anywhere, but employment was extremely hard to find, and food was scarce. I remember listening to some of their stories, which, no matter how accurate, were intriguing to a youngster.

True, there were many who drank any kind of alcohol they could come by, including what was known as canned heat, a waxed alcohol that came in a little can and was used to heat chafing dishes. These men would squeeze the alcohol out of the wax and drink it not only to get warm, but also to get a glow on to help them forget their miseries. When Grandma was criticized for giving them a dime because, as she was told, they would only use the money to buy canned heat, she told them that maybe they needed it more than food.

When a freight train stopped at the Santa Fe station near her house, these unfortunates flocked to Grandma's house in droves. Everyone was sure that somewhere there was some sort of secret trail marker, as there was always a line of men from the back steps to the front sidewalk waiting to be given a little work and a "sangwich." I say a "little" work because it was a rule with Grandma that no one ate without doing something to earn it. This was to help them keep their dignity, rather than for the good it would do Grandma's backyard, which was just a little piece of dirt with nothing but weeds and a small shed.

Grandma Noonie, and of course many like her, were the forerunners of places like St. Mary's Dining Hall and the other charitable havens which exist today. Mealtime was a regular ritual. As each man came to the door and asked for something to eat, Grandma Noonie told him it would be a few minutes and that while he waited, he should pick some weeds in the yard.

If one of the men became too serious about the work, Grandma would interrupt her "sangwich" making and lean out the back door to tell him he should leave a little work for the next man.

Grandma Noonie's philosophy was that it didn't matter who a person was or where he came from, that person was entitled to be treated with respect. That and many other rules for living were written in her dilapidated, yellow-covered book she read with me before I went to sleep at her house.

We grandchildren were also a part of a larger, more distant charity. This was the distribution of funds to the various *michelachim* (collectors for the orphanages and *chaiders*, or Hebrew schools, in the Holy Land not yet known as the state of Israel), who came around from time to time to gather donations. These *michelachim* (angels, of a sort) would sometimes make a reservation at the house beforehand or would just arrive on the doorstep and expect something to eat if it was meal time or just a *gluzeleh taye* (little cup of tea) and cake if it was not. Many of them were repeat customers and were known by name These men usually stayed at a boarding house near the Civic Auditorium.

Grandma sent a dollar bill in response to the dozens of mailed requests, which often included a souvenir to obligate the recipient to donate something. Ours was the job of writing the brief notes she enclosed with each remittance. This is what she had us write: "Thank you for the blessings. Please do not send anymore ties, calendars, key chains" or whatever else they would send as guilt offerings. "We send a little to everyone. (Signed) Mrs. M. Corren and family." These notes had to be written before we received our hot chocolate and *mandal brot – choomish broit* as Grandma called it – a flat cake with almonds that was twice baked. It was so hard that it was perfect for dunking. The Italians make a similar delicacy, biscotti.

Grandma was also notorious for overbidding herself in the synagogue during the annual auctioning of the Aliyahs (honor of blessing the Torah before and after the reading, the opening of the Arc, the dressing of the Torah, etc.) during the New Year holidays. She would bid on these various honors so as to give them out to her children and grandchildren, but, when she thought the bidding had not gone high enough, she overbid herself to try to keep the bidding open. She would then be loudly admonished by the auctioneer not to do so. Her equally loud reply, so that all could hear, was that the congregation was not bidding enough.

The Stockton that Greeted Mendel

To paint a verbal picture of the Stockton Grandpa Mendel found when he arrived in 1901, we must first look at this very brief history:

At that time Stockton was a small city which had been known by many names: Tuleburg, Gas City and Mudville but the founder, Capt. Charles Weber, decided on the name Stockton to honor Commodore Robert F. Stockton, who had once saved his life.

On July 23, 1851 the city received its charter from the State Of California and was already about 50 years old when Grandpa Mendel arrived. Its location on a waterway, as well as its proximity to the mines, made it one of the most important supply bases for the California Mother Lode, attracting many immigrants adept at the art of doing business. Some merchants – many of them peddlers, as was Grandpa Mendel – did well enough to move on to larger cities.

This must have been an exciting time for a newcomer with the vision and energy to seize upon the many opportunities afforded in this budding community. For someone as gregarious by nature as Mendel, it must also have been an exhilarating experience.

At the same time, it must have been overwhelming for that newcomer, in this case Grandpa Mendel, to be thrown into a society which was completely foreign, with customs and attitudes he had never before experienced.

In an interesting anecdote passed along by the Davidson family, the principal reason the family stayed in the United States was the national sport: baseball. This is the story: Herschal Davidson, the husband of Schiferra Corren Davidson, Mendel's oldest sister, had initially come to Stockton with his daughter Anne and young son Sam, but after a short stay decided that America was not the place for him and his family. It was simply not religious enough, so he decided to pack them all up and return to Russia. Anne agreed with whatever her father wanted, but Sam had discovered baseball and told his father that he would run away rather than return to Russia. The rest is history.

This crucial decision, although seemingly frivolous, would greatly affect the future of the Corren family, since it was on a future ship that Mendel arrived with his older sister, sent for by her husband, Herschal, whose decision to return home was thwarted by his son's love of baseball.

The photos on the next page are from the book *Stockton in Vintage Postcards* courtesy of the author, Alice van Ommeren. They show Stockton as Mendel would have seen it when he arrived in 1901.

It was a blossoming city established some fifty years earlier by miners, trappers and others, including business people, who recognized its favorable position on a waterway very close to the mines.

WATERFRONT AT STOCKTON. "Two transcontinental railroads and numerous steamship lines served the bustling metropolis of the Upper San Joaquin Valley." The head of the deepwater channel was filled with riverboats carrying freight and passengers between Stockton and San Francisco.

MAIN STREET, LOOKING EAST. This card, postmarked in 1908, provides a view of Main Street looking east from Center Street. On the left side of the street up a block is the "IXL," a men's clothing store operating on the corner of El Dorado Street and Main Street since 1884. In 1910, the clothing store moved into the ground floor of the Hotel Stockton building.

THE LEVEE. This postcard of the "Levee" offers an early view of Weber Avenue, facing west. This card, postmarked in 1905, is from the era of "undivided back" postcards, during which the address was the only writing permitted on the back. Notice the delivery wagons parked next to the waterfront sheds. The Sperry Flour Mill buildings stand in the background.

MEL CORREN

Grandpa's Religious Affiliations

The first of our extended family to emigrate was Rabbi/Cantor Herman Davidson who in a way was responsible for the future arrival of the Herschal Davidson and Mendel Corren families. Cantor Davidson was an opera singer who came over with a Russian touring troupe in the latter part of the 19th century and decided to jump ship in San Francisco where he was informed that they needed a Cantor in Stockton. He applied and became the religious leader of Rhyim Ahovim Synagogue (either the first or second Hebrew congregation founded west of the Rockies) but after many years was let go due to that congregation's desire to become even more reform, making Herman's accent and traditional ways unsuitable.

He then moved to Manteca married and settled down until the turn of the century when he was again called upon to lead a new orthodox congregation, called Ahavas Aachim.

Of course the cemetery of the reform temple, Rhyim Ahovim, the oldest documented Jewish burial grounds west of the Rockies, was not kosher enough for this new orthodox *shul* (a small temple/school in the *shtels* of eastern Europe) so it created one of its own, and in it is buried Cantor Davidson and his wife.

Grandpa Mendel joined Ahavas Achem on his arrival and remained a member until the late 1930s when he joined the newer orthodox congregation Adas Yeshuran, This congregation was established on Fremont Street in 1914 according to a document signed by the then California Secretary of State Frank Jordan, a copy of which is on display in the lobby of Rhyim Ahovim, now known as Temple Israel.

The congregation of Ahavas Aachim met for many years in various places, such as Redman's Hall and other venues, before moving into its own place of worship. I remember as a child attending Ahavas Aachim in a converted house on Park Street, where I sat through the service with Grandpa Mendel and my dad. My one vivid recollection of the place are the huge palm trees which stood in front.

Though Grandpa Mendel joined Adas Yeshurun in his later years, he is buried in the cemetery of his original *shul*, Ahavas Aachim. Since his burial in 1939, most of his descendants have been buried there as well. It became a

tradition which continues to this day. In fact, so many of our family's dead are buried there, I sometimes refer to it as "Our Town."

The cemetery site was originally owned by the Catholic Church and bought through Father O'Connor who had planned to build a home for the aged there. But when it proved too small for his purpose, however, he sold it to Ahavas Aachim, which consecrated it as its cemetery. Father O'Connor was the priest whose name is attached to the senior citizen housing in North Stockton, known as O'Connor Woods, where many of our friends and family now live.

Throughout the years, Adas Yeshuran had a series of "rabbis" who were really *malamuds* (teachers). They taught *chaider* (Hebrew school) classes and performed services along with the lay leaders. Then, in the mid thirties a real rabbi, Benjamin Cohen, came to Adas Yeshurun. Everyone loved him, even a large group from the reform temple. Even we children enjoyed attending *chaider* after he came to town. He was not only a learned rabbi, but had a beautiful voice, and he became fast friends with our whole family, especially Grandpa Mendel. They would sing together, and on the high holidays they formed a choir made up principally of members of the Corren family. There were six Correns in the original choir. In subsequent years, my brother Hillard joined for a total of seven.

I was supposed to be bar mitzvahed by Rabbi Cohen, but he had to leave town for a brief period, so I was instead bar mitzvahed by a well respected lay member of the local orthodox community named Mr. Shmul Todresic. What I remember most about studying for my bar mitzvah in the Todresics' cozy kitchen was the wonderful chicken soup. My bar mitzvah was nothing like the

bar and bat mitzvahs in the reform synagogues today. It took place in Adas Yeshurun, the orthodox *shul* on Fremont Street, and it was merely me, sandwiched into a normal Shabbas service, standing between the rabbi and my grandfather. I had been called up during the weekly reading of the Torah, and, while being coached, corrected and prodded by the elders, recited my portion. Then, having finished my part of the service, I made my little speech (no ad libs in those days) and sat down. Sure, I got many gifts, but did I have my hour on the *bema* (pulpit) like bar and bat mitzvah kids have now? No!

The Adas Yeshurun *shul* flourished during the 1920s, and, in the 1930s was even more popular among the Jewish people in Stockton than the Temple, because there were more Eastern European Jews immigrating during the early twentieth century, and they considered Reform Jewry to be what they termed, *Dietchesha Yuhudim* (German Jews, who were, in fact the founders of the Temple). Many of the families of these early founders moved away from Stockton in later years.

After World War II, the *shul* was remodeled, which called for a re-consecration. A parade marched about three blocks to the *shul*, where we

all reentered the building and began a little praying and a whole lot of partying.

The *shul* began losing its importance shortly after this and declined until it was finally dissolved after a devastating fire.

The land for Rhim Ahovim, as already mentioned, the oldest continually operating Jewish cemetery west of the Rockies, was given to the congregation in 1851 by Capt. Charles Weber, the founder of the city. Because of its designation as an historical landmark, it was rescued from its rundown condition in the 1960s by Bea Schwartz who worked tirelessly to get the funds to improve the grounds and create an endowment fund for its future care.

Ahavas Aachim cemetery was originally administered by Mr. Bauble, and after his death by my dad, Sam Corren, and Mr. Baumel's son-in-law, Morrie Stein, followed by my brother, Hillard Corren. It is now being overseen by my cousin, Craig Corren, and a board of directors.

Note: Morrie Stein and his wife Faye had reserved the front two plots but later decided to be buried in Rhim Ahovim, now those two pieces of real estate will be my wife's and my "resting places."

For more information, refer to: "The History of San Joaquin County, California with Biographical Sketches," Historic Record

Company, Los Angeles, CA-1923; and "Early Stockton Jewry and Its Cantor, Rabbi Herman Davidson" by Reva Clar, The Western States Jewish Historical Quarterly, January-April 1973.

This along with The Kantrowitz Family Chronicle, an unpublished account and Family Tree, created by Reva Clar, Harriet "Tasha" Davidson Stadtner, Daniel Peletz, and distributed only to family members has contributed much of the history I have included herein.

PHOTOS:

The original Adas Yeshurun choir including Rabbi Cohen and Grandpa Mendel, with four of his sons and grandson, Mel.

Parade to the shul celebrating the re-consecration of the remodeled shul.

Kantorowitz Family History Chronicle created by Reva Clar, Harriet, Tasha, Davidson Stadtner, Daniel Peletz.

Rabbi/Cantor Herman Davidson, the first of our extended family to arrive in America.

Cantor Davidson's headstone, Ahavas Aachim.

(Author's photos and others unknown)

Starting Out

When Mendel arrived in Stockton, he was set up with a horse and wagon to collect bottles, rags and other items for the Davidson Junk business, but this did not last long as he preferred to be in business for himself selling merchandise off of his own wagon.

At the time, the Jewish Agency was one of the organizations responsible for settling the Jewish immigrants arriving in great numbers from all over the world, predominantly Eastern Europe. It would supply the newcomer (the "greener") with a horse, wagon and goods to start a peddling business. The agency expected to be repaid when the immigrant got on his feet so that others could later benefit.

Mendel began his peddling career selling notions, and ended up with vegetables. A story goes that his wife, Noonie, refused to take anything left over from his vegetable cart because it belonged to the *ohrama mentshen* (poor people).

It never ceases to amaze me that after a year or so he had saved enough money to send to Russia for Noonie and their two baby sons. When Mendel left her in Poltova, they had one son, Harry. Neither of them realized she was pregnant. (Can you imagine how she must have felt when, after he left, she

discovered this bit of news?) Mendel also sent for his parents and brothers, Hillel and Abe, who would also settle in Stockton.

Try to picture Mendel loading his wagon, hitching it to a horse, and traveling from Stockton to the small encampments in the Sierra foothills to sell his goods and buy furs and other items to sell back in Stockton. It's a scene right out of one of Sholem Aleichem's stories.

It's hard to conceive of the hardships, loneliness and monotony he must have suffered, but, on balance, I try to imagine what it must have meant to him and the other men to live in an open society, with all the possibilities for personal growth and achievement that lay before them. It required devotion, hard work and a vision, but it was worth the effort when they found that proverbial pot of gold at the end of the rainbow.

PHOTO:

Capt. Tom Petersen, a trapper and Mendel.
According to the note on the back, they are holding
sacks of mink pelts (Photographer unknown)

Going Into Business

At this point we have Mendel, Noonie, Harry and Sam living in Stockton. Later would come six more children: Sadie, Rose (Rosie), Meyer (Mike), Maurice, Israel (Izzy) and, after a hiatus of several years, Allen Liberty (Alleyboy). His middle name was given to him because he was born during World War I and was named after the Liberty Bond. The

nickname, Alleyboy, was due to his being a surprise in a family already established (he was initially thought to have been a tumor) and thus

was allowed to run more wild than his older brothers and sisters.

Mendel's early days of peddling enabled him to send to Russia for his mother, Esther (for whom my sister, who died as an infant, was named) and his father, Moshe (for whom I am named). Moshe and Esther are buried in Oakland, CA, as they came over at an advanced age and

made their new home with one of Mendel's brothers who lived there at the time.

As difficult as Mendel's first years were, the carrot was always the same: To make it in America as an American. According to family lore, April 18, 1906, was the day everything changed for Mendel, and for all our futures as well.

That was the day of the great San Francisco earthquake and fire. As a result of the devastation, fire-damaged furniture and goods were brought up to Stockton on barges, where it was sold or auctioned in the waterfront warehouse at the head of the channel across from the future Hotel Stockton.

Mendel and another peddler friend, Mr. Cleinmann, heard about the sale, formed a partnership, pooled their money and bought some of the merchandise. They rented a small store from Ms. Shrieky on the

Southeast corner of Washington and San Joaquin Streets and started a business appropriately named "Cleinmann and Corren."

The two former peddlers operated this store together for several years until the Correns, being more prolific, began bringing their sons, beginning with Harry and my father, Sam, into the business. Mr. Cleinmann then moved on to Southern California. (Many years later, my brother Hillard and I, Mendel Corren's grandsons, bought a game set from Cleinmann Furniture Mfg. Co. for our small store and discovered that the owner was Joe Cleinmann, the son of Grandpa's original partner.)

Grandpa Mendel was also in a group that bought and sold real estate with whatever money it could gather to invest. The group dabbled mainly in ranches, which they bought and quickly sold if a small profit was in the offing. They didn't hold anything long enough to really capitalize on the investment. This was before the advent of income and capital gains taxes, so whatever they gained from the sale, they pocketed.

When Grandpa was interviewed by the *Stockton Independent* newspaper regarding the new income tax law, he was reported to have said, "As long as they don't take what I came over here with, it's all right with me."

PHOTOS:

Grandma Noonie's mother, Leah Metz, Meyer (Mike), Rosie, Grandma Noonie, Harry, Sam and Sadie

Mendel in front of his first store

Invoice from Cleinmann & Corren

Uncle Harry and my father, Sam

Grandpa Mendel and the captain on a ferry to a Delta Island Farm

(Photographers unknown)

My Mother's Family

Dora and Grandpa Hilly Levine were my mother's parents. The Levines, like the Correns, to whom they were related, also came from a *shtetl* somewhere between the towns of Poltava and Chernigov in the Ukraine. They, as previously mentioned, left Russia earlier and settled for a short time in England, where the first of their nine children was born.

The family was not affluent. Grandpa Hilly (called Henry in America) had a tobacco shop and other kinds of businesses. (My mother always lamented the fact that someone took the cigar store Indian that had been in front of the store). The family lived from hand to mouth, and the children, as they became older, contributed to the family's income.

Many members of the family were plagued with depression, and some to the extreme. I myself suffered a bout in my forties when Howard, our older son, went to Russia to study. It was during the Cold War and the political climate was tense. I had such fears that I became depressed. At first I denied it, but while dining at the home of my good friend and doctor, Ed Swillinger, he recognized the symptoms and suggested to Harriet that I make an appointment. He prescribed a medication called Sinaquan, which helped me a great deal, but I believe it was his suggestion I do a course of biofeedback that led me out of it. This was a series of sessions with a psychologist who hooked me up to a machine that buzzed loudly when I was nervous and depressed, but became less noisy as I calmed down. By the time I finished the course, I could control my tense emotions and render the machine silent, or nearly so. I mastered this after eight sessions.

I practiced this technique some years later on a visit to Paris. We were on our way to visit the Catacombs when I tripped over a tree screen on the sidewalk and fell to the pavement, protecting my face with my hands. I told my wife, Harriet, that I was all right except for my wrists, which cushioned the impact of the fall.

I got up, dusted myself off, and, feeling no pain at that moment (I must have been in shock), continued down the winding stairway to the underground cavern which housed all the bones.

I was fine until we reached the bottom, where we huddled in a very small, dark and musty holding room before entering the tunnel which you must traverse before exiting at another winding staircase. There was no way to go back up the staircase because it was impossible to go against the one-way traffic coming down.

As I stood in this little chamber, the shock from the fall must have worn off. I was suddenly overcome by claustrophobia and began to perspire and feel faint. I felt even woozier at the prospect of fainting and having to be carried out. It was then that I began to draw on what I had learned those many years before in biofeedback therapy. I drew myself up against the wall and began to measure my breaths, and gradually I relaxed to the point I not only went through the tunnel of skulls but spent the rest of the day sightseeing, although my wrists and forearms hurt like crazy.

Back to the Levines: Grandma Dora and Grandpa Hilly had nine children: Sam, Ida, Annie, Mayme, Sadie, Goldie, Bessie, Jack, and Lilah. They all lived in various places outside of Stockton. We didn't have as much contact with them as with the Correns, but a few memories stand out in my mind:

Uncle Sam was well known as the head bartender at the Fresno Hotel. His oldest son, Bert, who was stationed in Alaska was among the first casualties of World War II. I visited with two of his other sons, George and Myron, during WWII in Paris.

Auntie Ida married Benny Lazaras, a colorful Scotsman, who had an automotive glass shop in Delano where he loved to show us kids how to cut and make things out of glass. We still have tumblers made of White Horse Scotch bottles.

Our family often went to their house in Delano to celebrate Thanksgiving, and what made the visit the most fun was sleeping in cousin Hille's top bunk and going next door to the glass shop and listening to Uncle Benny tell stories in his slightly Scottish accent.

We also learned to eat sukiyaki at a Japanese restaurant in Delano that was owned by a friend of Uncle Ben's. Who knew that just a few years later, after the attack on Pearl Harbor, these folks would be removed to a relocation center?

Auntie Mayme was an excellent

seamstress who worked in department and dress stores as a sales and/or alteration lady. Before she married, she often came to our house from Fresno. During her visit she would make great things out of cloth for us. Once, when I was 10, she made me a "smoking jacket" out of maroon velvet and black silk.

Auntie Bessie married Abe Sclarow, an engineer who worked on one of the first bridges from Minneapolis to Saint Paul. They had a son and two daughters, Marshall, Eileen and Donna Lee. Eileen was stricken with multiple sclerosis as a young child, but she graduated from college and worked all her life despite debilitating handicaps of speech and mobility.

Donna Lee, Aunt Bessie's youngest daughter, was named – as was my sister, Dora Lee, and our cousin, Doreen Lee – after their mutual grandmother, Dora, who died shortly before each of them was born.

Uncle Jack was in World War I and had been in a gas attack from which he suffered what we now know as post traumatic stress disorder. As a result he suffered from severe depression.

In spite of this disability, he rose to manager of the men's clothing department at Roos Brothers in Oakland. He was such a classic dresser that I can't remember ever seeing him without a coat and tie.

Auntie Sadie Michaels with whom I had dinner the night I met Harriet was divorced and had a daughter, Shirley, who grew up with a family near Grandma Dora's house. They were members of the Christian Science Church, which aroused my curiosity because it was so different from my religion. Shirley later married Walter Reinthaler, converted

to his Catholic religion and they raised a devout family. We have had many good times with the Reinthaler family over the years.

PHOTOS:

The Levine family in Duluth before my mother was born
Grandpa Hillie and Grandma oDr
(Photographers unknown)
Scotch bottle glass made by Uncle Benny
Uncle Benny and cousin Hillel.
Me with Auntie Mayme
Harriet, me, Walter, Shirley. Florence and Hillard
(Author's photos)

My Mother, Goldie

Goldie Carrie Levine, was the sixth daughter of Hillie (Henry) and Dora Levine who came to California from Duluth , Minnesota, in 1918, to visit their relatives, the Correns, and to see about moving here.

On that trip, Goldie met my father, Sam, and a few years later, when her family returned for a third visit, they began a courtship. A wonderful love affair developed that we kids have always considered a great influence on our relationships with our own spouses.

My parents loved to travel even before it was fashionable. They went all over the country by car; sometimes with us kids and sometimes just the two of them. Dad would drive and mom would knit. In later years, they went to more exotic places around the world.

Goldie's passion for travel was so strong that after dad passed away, she took Harriet and me to Europe, then Libby and Hillard to Israel, and later took Denny and Doralee to Asia. Then, on her eightieth birthday she took us all on a cruise through the Panama Canal.

These initial trips offered by our mother gave our family the urge to see the world. Harriet and I have visited my friends from WW II in London and Paris. We then ventured farther afield: Asia, the Middle East, North and South America, as well as other places in Europe.

Hillard and Libby would go in the summer and, since no one wanted a decorator in the house between Christmas and the first of the year, Harriet and I would leave often on Christmas Eve and stay away for about two weeks or so.

One memorable trip was to Bilbao, Spain, where we arrived the day before the famous museum, designed by Frank Gehry, was about to open. The Haggin Museum in Stockton wrote a letter indicating Harriet was a docent, and when we arrived and presented our "credentials" we were given passes to the Press Day opening.

Mother remained young in style, humor and philosophy well into her nineties.

PHOTOS:

Goldie Levine Corren
Mother at her 85th birthday party
(Photographers unknown)

My Father, Sam Corren

Sam Corren, the second oldest in the Mendel Corren family, set out from an early age to become a business man. At  the age of 19, after helping his father and older brother, Harry, in the used furniture store, he furthered the scope of the Correns' business by opening his own new furniture store that would later create more opportunities for the fledgling family business. Dad, however, was more than just a businessman, he was a person who reached out to others when they needed help and was an active participant in both the Jewish and local community alike.

As a youngster he was an early member of the De Molay Lodge here in Stockton and as a 32nd degree Mason sponsored me into the Stockton Lodge that later merged with Morning Star.

He was a member of the State Savings and Loan Association board of directors, and after his death I succeeded him.

His obituary, except for the fact it didn't mention he was a father who taught by example, said it all.

PHOTO:

Sam Corren (Photographer unknown)
Dad's obit from The Stockton News (courtesy of Sam Mathews of The Tracy Press

Herb's Squirrel Cage
BY HERB OF HERB'S SURPLUS

Sam Corren died last week. His passing is a genuine loss to our entire community because he was a man who was devoted to helping his fellow man, and his only criterion on giving help was that someone be in need.

Usually, you know, charitable activities are directed along religious lines: Catholics help Catholics, Methodists help Methodists, Lutherans help Lutherans, and so forth. Sam Corren was a Jew who was deeply attached to his faith, but that did not limit his sphere of activities. Any man in need, whatever his religion or color could get a helping hand from him. His funeral attested to this. People from all walks of life gathered there to honor his memory. As many non-Jews were there as were Jews. Ministers from many other faiths attended. People from all the racial and national groups that make up Stockton's wonderful population gathered there. Old people, young people, government and business leaders, just plain people, representatives of every strata of our community, all gathered to mourn his death. Truly, he was one of the great men of Stockton. May he rest in peace.

Liberty Furniture Co.

Harry and Sam worked with their father for several years at M. Corren and Sons Used Furniture Store until my father, Sam, decided to branch out on his own in a *new* furniture store. So in 1918, with the blessings of his father, he opened Liberty Furniture Company on South Hunter Street, across from the fire station and

public library. He named the store after the liberty bonds of World War I which were being sold to aid the war effort.

As luck would have it, this small store was located next to the Ofis Bar, owned by Harry Arbios and Pete Dellasandro. They were involved with the Wool Growers Association, so the Ofis was a gathering place for the Basque sheep herders, the mainstay of the wool trade in the area.

Sam hit it off with these folks, and as a result the Liberty Furniture Company began handling supplies for the sheep herders, such as crooks for herding, twine, sheep dip, lanterns, canvas water bags, marking materials, etc.

This created a whole new business opportunity for the Correns, because many of the Basque families who operated hotels and dining rooms became customers for furniture, bedding and window coverings for their businesses, as well as for their own homes. Note: Due to the quality and quantity of the Basque family style meals, these hotels became favorite dining places for the general population, as well as the herders and their families.

Then, in 1926 came an offer from Miss Shrieky, who owned the property where Mendel and Harry's used store was located, to build a very large single building which would occupy half of the block at 136-148 South San Joaquin Street, the northeast corner of which was occupied by M. Corren and Sons.

This proposal for a new and larger store was more than the used furniture business could support, so they asked Sam to rejoin them and create a "new and used" furniture store. This consolidation would accomplish two things: It would satisfy Sam's desire to deal in new furniture, which he had proven could be successfully done, and, it would make it possible for the family to work together in one location.

Sam closed the Liberty store and returned to the original business with his father and older brother, but this consolidation was still not enough to fill and pay the rent and expenses on the large building Miss Shrieky was intending to build, so Sam convinced Mr. Arbios and the Wool Growers Association to rent space from them in the new building. For many years, the offices of the Wool Growers Association were located right smack in the middle of M. Corren and Sons, separating the new furniture department from the used. The sheep camp supply department took up a whole section of the basement which, of course, would be referred to today as the lower level. This meant much to the future of M. Corren and Sons, as the Basque community supported the business personally as well as commercially.

We were invited to and attended many "Mountain Oyster" parties. Two of them stand out. The first with my dad who knew and introduced me to the Basque community. The second with my brother Hillard when Jean Cubiburu invited us to his annual bash at the California Hotel owned by the Alustiza family. Jean acquainted us with the bota bag. Hillard and I were very green (even greener after the party). We hadn't expected to drink as much wine as we did, but the pros passed the bota bag around and counted until you couldn't hold anymore or the bag was empty. To this day we don't know how we survived that night, but the next year we learned to drink like the old timers.

Other Basque families that owned restaurants were the Ospitals (The Villa Basque), the Idiartes (The Basque Hotel), and Teresa Moriones: (The Wool Growers) to name a few. They all served a set menu, and if you left hungry, shame on you!

Those early friendships have continued throughout the generations. The plaque at the entrance of Harry Corren Park in Spanos Park, proposed by the Reverend Bob Hailey, says it all.

PHOTOS:

My dad, Sam Corren, in front of his store, Liberty Furniture (Photographer unknown)

Photo of Harry Corren Park and the Dedication Plaque at the Park in Spanos Park (Google: Harry Corren Park, Stockton)

M. Corren and Sons

Mendel's oldest sons, Harry and Sam, were later included in the business that became known as M. Corren and Sons. As the years passed, their brothers – Meyer, Maurice, Izzy, and Allen (Alleyboy) – joined the business as well. (An interesting anecdote: Mail often came to the store addressed to "McCorren and Sons." Grandpa Mendel would again note that an Irishman had named him at Ellis Island).

Early on a drayman was hired. His name was Mottie, and he was great with horses, a good deliveryman and a crackerjack at repairing and refurbishing old cast iron stoves.

Others were hired, as well. When I was young Lena Pellegri was the woman who took care of all things "office." She was not only great in that capacity, but in the store was like a mother hen to us kids.

I must remember to mention Bill, who came to work when the horse and wagon was still the mode of delivery and stayed on until the 1950s. He was afflicted with epilepsy and always contended he was hooked up to an electric current triggered by forces on the White House lawn. He also claimed that the only thing that could save him was Pepsi Cola. Another of his idiosyncrasies was that he could not throw away a nail, screw or any other fastener from a crate that he unpacked, and since all merchandise came in wooden crates in those days, you can imagine how many containers of bent nails, screws, etc., were discovered after he left the firm.

When he lost his health, Bill went to live on the State Farm in Stockton, where people who no longer could manage on their own were able to live and work in a protected, productive environment. These facilities were later closed when medicines became available for the treatment of these folks. Unfortunately no one foresaw that those who needed these medications would discontinue taking them once they felt in control.

The first week after Bill moved there, he came to the store for a visit. It was about the time of day that the awnings had to be rolled down against the sun so my dad asked him to do the honors as had been his former custom. He looked my dad square in the eye, spit his customary dry spit, and asked, "Who's crazy, Sam? You or me?" It was the last time he was ever asked to lift a hand after his retirement.

In the early years, when Grandpa Mendel had a few extra dollars, he would go to all the auctions nearby and buy whatever struck his fancy. He bought beautiful old Victorian furniture, old bronze clocks, china and artifacts of all kinds. He bought dozens of Edison phones, old phonographs and Edison tubes (records). The collection included recordings of Enrico Caruso, famous cantors, Al Jolson and other vaudevillians and teams, such as Gallagher and Shean.

All these acquisitions were stacked up in the loft of the old barn behind the family home, where the horses had been kept during the drayage years. Uncle Harry told how when they were young, the Corren boys moved some of the heavier pieces of antique furniture from the second-floor hay loft by pushing them out the door and allowing them to smash down to the ground. Years later, many of these pieces would have commanded handsome prices.

The surviving antiques and collectibles were moved to what was called the "New Warehouse" at 518 South San Joaquin Street where we youngsters – ostensibly hired by our grandfather to keep the antiques dusted and the dead flies off the white china – created havoc with many of these possessions. We raced the angels, devils, knights and animals around the platforms on the top of the old clocks, threw china, used records as Frisbees (before we even knew about actual Frisbees), and generally made a mess of things, all the while collecting five dollars a week.

The business prospered, and by the time the Depression of the 1930s came along, Grandpa Mendel and his sons had built a reputation for fairness and quality, along with one other important ingredient: friendliness. This attribute became their motto and part of the firm's name: "M. CORREN AND SONS: The Friendly Furniture Store."

To this day women remember that when they became engaged, a miniature Lane cedar chest was presented to them and when they became mothers a little bootie with a bouquet was delivered to their hospital room – with a card from *The Friendly Furniture Store*. Others recall Mendel or one of the six brothers at M. Corren and Sons telling

them to just take the bed or stove or whatever home and pay when and as they could. These families paid off their debts as soon as they could and have never forgotten the trust and kindness.

Most sales at the Correns were made on a handshake. It was good practice for the customers who needed help, as well as for the store, because the offspring of many of these folks became future

customers. This is what made the business successful and saw it through the rough times of the Depression, proving Uncle Harry's favorite adage that if you "throw your bread upon the water, it will come back as sandwiches."

Grandpa and Grandma's home was about ten blocks south of the store, and Grandma Noonie's table was set every noon for whoever might come to the house for lunch. She could count on at least one or two of her sons, and often a road salesman, to arrive for whatever she was serving.

When the "boys," as Grandma called her sons, brought the road salesmen home for lunch

and the conversation got heavy, particularly political, one of Grandma's favorite admonishments was *"Vinsigerer geredt und mer gehgesun!"* ("More eating and less talking!") Another was, *"De tsung is a schverd."* ("The tongue is a sword.") This meant that what you say must be measured in terms of how it may be hurtful.

Two of my uncles – Uncle Mike and Uncle Allen – went into the Army, and three of us grandsons also served – Hillard in the Navy, and Irving and me in the Army. There was such *esprit de corps* in the family that Uncle Mike and Uncle Allen continued to receive their regular store wages until they returned home and to work.

The Correns had many friends and customers in Stockton's Japanese community, and when they were relocated in the hysteria created by Pearl Harbor, a section of the warehouse at 518 South San Joaquin Street was set aside as a storage area for their belongings. It was strictly off limits, and remained so until the owners returned after the war to reclaim their property.

Hillard's and my experience in the furniture business began on a part-time basis during school,

MEL CORREN

then after World War II we went to work in earnest. I studied interior design and began doing that work in the store, ultimately creating an interior decorating department. Hillard worked with Uncle Allen in the appliance store next to the parking lot, selling merchandise, as well as in the office next door, where he learned the rudiments of business, skills that would later prove germane to our own successful partnership, The Brothers.

At M. Corren and Sons, all major national and Jewish holidays were a reason to take the day off, as well as an excuse to have a dinner. Store holidays were celebrated at restaurants such as Raffanti's, later known as Bruno and Lena's. Jewish holidays, of course, were celebrated in the early days at my grandparents' and later in our own homes.

At Christmas and New Year's, a large buffet table laden with food and drink was set up in the middle of the store for customers and staff alike. This repast was catered by Gaiia Delucchi's Delicatessen, which had – and has – no equal.

In 1939, Grandpa Mendel, founder and sole owner of M. Corren & Sons, passed away while visiting his sister, Schiffera, at her

beach home in Ocean Park, California. The cause was diagnosed as a heart attack since he suffered from angina, but as was grandma's custom with names and the like, she declared the cause to be acute indigestion, saying she could have cured him if he had only stayed home. This was an ongoing thing with them - he liked to go and she liked to stay.

Shortly after Grandpa's death, Grandma found herself at the family lawyer's office turning her inheritance of the business over to her six sons as equal partners. This did not sit well with her two daughters nor their husbands. The reason was never revealed why Grandma did this. However, I believe there were two possibilities. It was the way families did it in the old country, leaving the inheritance only to the sons and letting the daughters be taken care of by their husbands. Or that Grandma Noonie, having had a business upbringing, realized the store, although profitable, had six partners and the inevitable act of buying the daughters out would adversely affect the business.

This, of course, created a rift in the family which was assuaged during WWII when Aunt Sadie and Uncle Ernest, San Franciscans, looked after my brother, Hillard, a sailor, stationed at Treasure Island during WWII. After that healing process the business continued for forty more years, until 1978 during which time old wounds were, from all intent and purposes, healed and or forgotten.

Grandpa Mendel's obituary, which appeared in *The Stockton Record*, spoke of his coming from Russia to this country at the turn of the century, establishing a successful and enduring business with his six sons, and contributing greatly to the City of Stockton.

PHOTOS:

Mendel and his six sons: (Front row: Harry, Mendel, Sam) (Back row: Mike, Izzy, Maurice and Allen)

Store circa 1928, '40-50, '60's until closing

Grandpa Mendel just before his death (Photographers unknown)

Grandpa's obituary (The Stockton Record)

Ad celebrating the store's 42nd anniversary (The Stockton Record)

.

The above donor's plaque on display in The Haggin Museum, along with this photo of a faded check from Mr. A.P. Giannini's BANK OF ITALY, puts Grandpa Mendel in very good company.

At Grandma's and Grandpa's House

When I was young and my parents were away, or wanted to sleep late on a Sunday morning, they left me at my grandparents' house for the weekend. Grandma Noonie seemed very happy about this arrangement. Having had eight children, the youngest only six years older than me, she considered me just an extension of her immediate family.

For me, it was more than a sleepover, as during these weekends she taught me many things that have had a great influence on my life. She taught me the morning and evening prayers and explained that although they were the Hebrew ones ascribed to us as Jews, there were many more in other languages which preached the same lesson - tolerance.

While she spoke English quite well, albeit with a little accent, Grandma Noonie always spoke to me in Yiddish and expected me to answer in the same. I've thanked her on many occasions for persevering in this endeavor, because this knowledge has benefitted me often during my lifetime when confronted with an unknown language and someone Jewish arrived on the scene.

She also raised moral issues, many of them codified in her collection of books that were laid out on the table and the buffet. They were books having to do with health as well as living a good life, a life in which ethics played a great part. I didn't want our discussions to end.

A lesson I have remembered all my life, particularly when making a list of invitees, is the story she told me about the man who, before he rose to a prominent position in the community, shared his life and times with his best friend who remained a regular tradesman. But when it came time to make a list for the ball which celebrated his rise, he ignored his friend. This, of course, caused much animosity and later, when this man also became important, he contributed to the downfall of his disloyal friend.

Grandma Noonie wanted me to appreciate the knowledge passed on to us by every nationality and creed so that I would not become a *kanyoka* (a word she concocted to describe one who follows only one creed to an extreme).

The wonderful meals and snacks she prepared were, by gourmet standards, very simple, but they were special treats for me. Even now, at 92 years of age, I am able to enjoy, in memory, the delightful tastes and smells that made her house such a special haven.

When the meals were *milchedich* (non-meat), they consisted of fish, vegetables, butter, eggs, milk and bread (the latter known to her as the "staff of life").

When the meal was *fleishadick* (with a meat dish), it could not be prepared or served with any milk product. These separations were proscribed by Biblical law: "Thou shalt not boil the kid in the mother's milk" – an example of compassion. For this reason she kept a strictly kosher house. She

used two sets of dishes and silverware, one for meat and the other for milk, and if a dish was despoiled by using it with the wrong ingredient, it was buried in the ground for a day.

Food at Grandma's house was anything but fancy, but to me it was – and has always remained in my mind – extra special. I've already described hamlettes and hot chocolate, but equally important were other delicacies, such as the *gebrutenze*, a chuck roast or similar inexpensive cut of meat which was kashered, meaning it had been brought home from the kosher butcher's (*shoechet's*) shop, rinsed several times and salted (to erase any taste of the meat), then placed in a roasting pan with garlic, onions, carrots and potatoes. It was then cooked until all the ingredients were scorched to the bottom of the pan – a delicacy the likes of which I have not eaten since those wonderful days. No one ever arose from the table and volunteered to wash the roasting pan.

Oh, how the big hamburger emporiums of today would love to get hold of the recipe for her most famous repast: the *kachlatin*, a true gem of a hamburger that I have tried in vain to have duplicated by restaurants and food stands. It was simply made with not-so-secret ingredients: bread crumbs, a beaten egg, chopped onion, and a small amount of ground beef, all squeezed into a patty and fried until well done, but the most important ingredient, Grandma's love, is no longer available. These dishes cannot be duplicated in a world which has moved on to fast-frozen, quick-dried, energy-efficient, super healthy, nonfat, and low-sugar foods.

Chicken was usually reserved for Shabbat. It was first used to make a rich broth, saved, and served later as an entree with carrots and celery. *Lauction* (egg noodles) or *canedlach* (matzo balls) would be added to the soup at the last minute. This soup is known as Jewish penicillin, and on many occasions it's been purported to have saved the lives of Jews and non-Jews alike. This was the era right on the cusp of this new and modern world, which, in the beginning technology made almost everything old fashioned every two or three years, and now seemingly every minute.

It was an all-too-short period in time, when a few conveniences were available but relatively simple living was still possible. My good fortune was to have lived my adolescence in this brief period between two eras, the first with advancements that made life easier and more enjoyable, and the second, which makes life virtually a dash through time. I reflect on this now as I write on this computer, an instrument capable of reaching around the world with its capacity to send e-mail, correct spelling errors, arrange and rearrange thoughts, keep track of activities and instantly locate information which, in earlier times, took days, weeks or even years to retrieve, if at all.

Much is said in praise of the progress that's been made in recent years concerning our ability to communicate, but, at the same time, it seems we are losing our ability to interact with one another. Often a couple, sitting across from one another in a restaurant, may be observed poking their fingers at a smart phone. The question which comes to mind is: Are they texting others not present, or one another?

The many familiar things in Grandma's house were, apart from their sentimentality, not of great value, but all the same when she moved to the duplex each of her children and grandchildren chose he or she wanted as a remembrance. The list began with the candelabra which was always on the dining room table next to the old, page crumpled book of the Sages (which I have previously referred to), the broken player piano and the walnut wall clock which belted out the hours.

The piece I selected was a small pressed glass candy dish. It was always filled with hard candies.

PHOTOS:

Back row: Jimmy Castle, unknown, Uncle Meyer (Mike),
Bottom row: Uncle Allen (Alleyboy), Irv, Auntie Sophie, Hillard and me
(L to R) Uncle Alleyboy, Irving, Uncle Harry, Hillard. Uncle Dan Levy (Arnold's father),
Uncle Izzy, and me on top
Grandma's candy dish now at our house
(Photos from author's collection)

MEL CORREN

Weekends at Grandma and Grandpa's

The weekends at Grandma and Grandpa's house were wonderful learning experiences in human nature. It was quite apparent, even to a youngster, that Grandpa and Grandma not only had different priorities, but also lived in different worlds. I remember vividly that when Grandpa and I were about to set off for the synagogue or the movies, just as we turned the knob to go out the front door, Grandma would begin to harangue him for something he forgot to do or something she just knew he was about to do wrong or forget to do altogether. This episode could last for as long as 15 minutes, and I can still see in my mind's eye Grandpa putting his weight first on one foot and then the other and repeating at every break, "Yes, Annuta" (his own special appellation) as he reached fervently for the door knob. Now, there has been speculation as to their actual relationship *vis a vis* romantic love, but Grandma was and continued to be a tall handsome woman, and they had eight children, so make of it what you will.

On days that for one reason or another we did not go to a movie, Grandpa and I would visit his cronies. The closest was the Joe Schwartz family at their grocery store a couple of blocks away, the "Blue Goose Market." There we would be treated to various delicacies off the shelves and the cases. Afterward, we would go upstairs, where they lived, and sing and play on the piano.

Joe Schwartz was a *Cohan*, a descendant of the ancient priests. When our son Howard was born – the first male child – we, as was the ancient custom, bought him back from Mr. Schwartz, acting in his capacity as a high priest, for a prescribed amount of money which was then donated to the synagogue.

Other times we went farther afield to Maishka Sweet's family where Grandpa and Maishka, a tenor in the *shul's* choir, would harmonize.

From these visits, I learned what real friendship was all about.

Staying over at my grandparents' on Sunday night meant that I would go to the Jackson school, just three blocks down, on Monday morning with

Uncle Alleyboy. As a result, I knew many of his classmates as well as the kids in the neighborhood. This meant I had the unique privilege of being included in the Southside as well as the Northside groups at the only high school in town. In this school, locale was a distinction which eclipsed race and religion. If you were from the Southside or Eastside of town, you were known as a Southsider or an Eastsider, but if you were from the North or West, you were known as a "400." (This old expression was coined because Mrs. Astor's ballroom could only accommodate 400 people). I was an "Everyman" and have always endeavored to be.

I loved to go across the street to the Bones' house, where they kept chickens in their yard and sold eggs. Mr. and Mrs. Bones were quite old, and he was very stooped, but they managed to entertain us kids by telling stories and letting us play with the glass eggs they used to train the hens to sit. I once squeezed one a little too hard and cut my hand. In those days accidents like that didn't result in a lawsuit.

Another wonderful adventure was strolling up and down the street, waiting for one of the neighbors to invite me in for home-baked cookies. My favorite invitation was from a neighbor who would beckon to me, then usher me into his dirt-floor half basement where his wife would serve me biscotti and he would hand me a small shot of sweet, homemade wine. My cousin Arnold also remembers having been treated to this. In this day and age, an event like this might easily make the newspapers.

Grandma and Grandpa's neighbors were immigrants with varied experiences who spoke their own native languages; however, they also all spoke English in their own limited way. They shared the same sense of now while trying to

make a future for themselves in their new environment. They were in the same boat, so to speak, and although at times they came up against very difficult obstacles, they pulled together like a big extended family, sharing and caring.

From them, I learned tolerance and the art of cooperation, and I also learned that being a neighbor meant not just living in the neighborhood, but interacting and participating.

On warm summer evenings, it was not unusual for as many as ten of us to sit on the front porch and talk, laugh, eat and generally have a good time. In that simpler era, there was little else to do besides visit with one another or go to a movie or event in town. Carnivals were very popular with the young set – there was a huge lot across from the nearby railway station, which was the usual site. Radio was still a novelty, although Grandma and Grandpa had an Atwater Kent in the living room. Later they got a Zenith, which could bring in short-wave reception from nearly every place on earth when the mood struck it. But in those days, the main mode of communication was, by necessity, mouth to ear, mouth to ear, mouth to ear – and the final telling was not always the same as the first.

The porch at my grandparents' house had wicker furniture, which we, in our teen years, demolished by pulling out strands and smoking them. The smoke was so strong it burned your eyes, to say nothing of your throat. The house and the porch seemed so large then, but every time I've gone by 35 E. Jefferson since it seems to have shrunk.

Auntie Rosie (sometimes separated and sometimes divorced from her husband Uncle Dan) and their son Arnold lived at times with Grandma. Rosie would create the most outrageous snacks in the middle of the night. One example: a slice of onion and a slice of tomato on garlic-rubbed rye bread. For a beverage, we were sent to the tavern – Dud's Place – on the corner to get a pitcher of suds (slang for beer). You could do that in those days with your own pitcher and no I. D. Today, I would be in juvenile hall and the barkeep would be up on charges.

From these everyday escapades, I learned that simple pleasures make for fond and lasting memories.

Sometimes when I stayed at Grandma's I was sent to the Bubba Leah's, grandma's mother, to clean up or help her do something at her little duplex. The Bubba Leah was quite eccentric. She spoke with a decided accent, had few or no teeth and taxied all over town. She carried a cane, which she banged ferociously when provoked or when she came in contact with her daughter, Grandma Noonie.

They got along like cats and dogs, and Grandpa Mendel created big-time tension by egging them on. Their relationship might have had to do with the fact – mentioned earlier – that in Russia the Bubba had farmed Grandma Noonie out to an uncle..

The Bubba was quite a character, but in her purse, wrapped in a handkerchief, she always had some of those tart, sugar-coated lemon drops, which could steal the heart of a young 'un.

I learned at an early age to respect and assist my elders.

There was an empty lot on the corner next door, the site of an automatic ice-dispensing hut. This was a small wooden building where the ice company stocked various-weight blocks of ice for use in ice boxes. When a customer inserted the proper combination of coins, the ice block would slide out, first through a burlap curtain, and then through a door that was pulled up manually. We considered this a very modern piece of machinery. Prior to that innovation, the ice man would ride down the street in a horse and wagon, and the people in the neighborhood would come out of their houses to greet him and buy whichever block of ice would fit in their ice box. It was as much a social experience as it was a commercial one. The same was true of the fruit and vegetable peddler, the knife and scissors sharpener, and the rags, bones, bottles and sacks collector (long before the current recycling craze, this was a way of making a living). In those days, most everyone either walked or was transported by horse or horse and wagon. Goods were also moved in the same way. This form of transportation

created a fuel byproduct that could be seen, and the perfume of which, although malodorous, was hardly even noticed (much like carbon monoxide today).

On the lot behind the house stood a large old barn. Horses had once been stabled there, but after the livery days, it became a warehouse for the antiques Grandpa Mendel collected. In later years, it and the lot in front became sites for houses. Alas, the once-majestic fig tree is gone, along with the ants that nourished themselves on its sap and fruit.

As it is with everything, nothing is the same in the old neighborhood. As I look back, all of these years have passed in the twinkling of an eye, and now, in the twilight of life, I've come to realize the amazing truth of Grandma Noonie's favorite expression:

"*Life is a dream.*"

PHOTOS:

Grandma and Grandpa
The "Southsiders" with the Bubba on the porch
The Bubba, grandma, Leah
Dad in front of the empty lot before the ice machine was installed
(From author's collection)

The Holidays

The memories of the holidays celebrated with the family at 35 East Jefferson Street remain so vivid and wonderful that it is impossible for me to select just one as the best or most enjoyable. With Rabbi Pinsker and Grandpa Mendel leading the group, we sang old Yiddish songs, Hebrew prayer songs and even modern American classics.

Grandma always claimed we were cousins of Irving Berlin (Isadore Baelin, in the old country). She even told us much about him and often asked me to write him so he would know where she was, but I never did. After he died and his personal information was released, some of which reflected what she had told me, I felt guilty that I hadn't obeyed her wishes. My thinking was that he might think we wanted something from him. Interestingly, when my granddaughter, Talia, graduated from the University of Michigan with a degree in musical comedy, her first job was as a swing backup for three female leads in the traveling musical *I Love a Piano*, featuring the songs of Irving Berlin!

§

On the holiday of Succot, we built a Succoh – a booth made of branches and laden with fruit from the harvest – where we gathered for evening meals during the holiday. Succot was a particularly enjoyable, laid-back celebration because it was very cozy and different from everyday life.

§

We also celebrated Christmas, since that was the day grandma and grandpa celebrated their wedding anniversary, for reasons unknown to me. Maybe it was because almost everyone else was celebrating on that day, so why not us?

§

When Rosh Hashona came around, we were treated to a new outfit by grandma, and each grandchild had a special shopping day. We met at the family store and went from there to the clothing stores on Main Street: Bravo and McKeegan, Yost Brothers, Threfall Brothers, Celayetta's and Sam Aaron's. We covered them all until we found the right outfit (I always liked a double breasted jacket and overcoat). The salesmen in the stores knew grandma and greeted her warmly, I suppose, with the hope that we would choose their offering.

I enjoyed clothes and loved to go through my uncles' closets and try on their outfits. They were very

fashionable dressers, as was Grandpa Mendel and when I grew a little, I asked them if I could have their old suits when they were finished with the. I remember the first time a suit of Uncle Izzy's - the sharpy of the sharpies - almost fit me and I had it cut down. It was a bold dark blue chalk-stripe, very fashionable in its day.

That suit is associated with an embarrassing remembrance that still makes me cringe when I recall it. I was in the eighth grade, and one night a week we had ballroom dancing classes at a children's dance studio called Snell's Bungalow.

Picture this: A 13-year-old boy in his uncle's dark blue chalk-stripe suit, a white silk scarf and a felt hat. That evening, while dancing, I felt I was the cat's meow. Later, however, when reality set in, I looked back on my dancing debut with the self-consciousness only a young person can relate to. It was several years before I could actually speak or laugh about it, although I must admit that it didn't stop me from taking my uncles' clothes to the tailor. Like my uncles and Grandpa Mendel, I was a young Dapper Dan.

Once while "shopping" for clothes in my uncles' closet I stumbled upon a jar full of cherries which tasted pretty darn good but shortly afterward when I was weaving across the room, Grandma Noonie found me and told me to never touch those brandied cherries again.

§

Passover Sedars were wild celebrations. The living room and sitting room, which had long since been joined by the removal of a common wall, created space for a table approximately 16 feet long built of boards and saw horses. It was set with all the Pesach symbols, as well as the *pesadecha* dishes and silver. These utensils had been stored during the year and now replaced the everyday ones for the eight days of the holiday. (In the Orthodox tradition, Passover is kept for eight days rather than the seven observed in the Reform movement, just in case there is a deviation in the calendar due to the fact that Jews are in many time zones because of the Diaspora; this accommodation is made for other holidays as well.)

What a glorious sight that table was, and how quickly it became a shambles!

At the Seder, Grandpa and the other elders sat leaning against pillows like kings, a ritual designed to distinguish our journey from former slaves to free people. The women took turns serving the Passover symbols as they were announced in the readings: The bitter herb - a bed of shredded horseradish root, to remind us of the bitterness of slavery; the *charosus* – a mixture of chopped nuts, apples and honey, to remind us of the sweetness of freedom; a chopped hard boiled egg in salt water, to remind us of the tears that were shed by those of us who were Jews in slavery; the lamb shank - an actual roasted shank, or substituted turkey neck or whatever - to remind us Jewish houses were passed over. The story goes that during the tenth plague, the blood of a lamb was smeared on the door frame of Jewish homes so that the Angel of Death would pass over it. Hence the name of the holiday.

The wine glasses were filled the necessary number of times during the reading of the *Hagadah*, the recounting of the hardships and ultimate release of Moses and the Children of Israel. The *fier kashes* (four questions) were recited by the youngest member of the family. The answers to those questions explain the meaning of Passover in historical terms and also serve as a guide for living our lives in freedom. The message as I saw it was that in freedom one must take responsibility for all of his or her choices with regard to everyday living.

Also meaningful for me was the story in which G–d, seeing the freed Israelites rejoicing as the Pharaoh's soldiers drowned in the returning waves of the sea, admonished them by asking whether those soldiers were not also of his making, his children as well. A powerful lesson, but when, if ever, will it be heeded?

After the meal, the service re-commenced. This included our thanks to G-d for deliverance from Egypt, the singing of songs and the consumption of more wine. At one point in the service, just before the after-dinner singing, the youngest child is instructed to open the door for the Prophet Elijah, who is supposed to visit each Jewish household on the night of the seder.

The glass of wine traditionally set for him in the center of the table is called to the attention of the little ones as an adult gently shakes the table. making the wine in the glass move ever so slightly. In later years, it seemed that whenever we expected to greet the Prophet Elijah, Uncle Alleyboy and Aunt Gertrude would be at the door. Their Seder always finished earlier and they often arrived just in time for the after-dinner entertainment.

Passover has always been an enjoyable and meaningful holiday for me because it is more than it seems on the surface. It is the foundation for the concept of freedom and tolerance Jews have espoused throughout the ages because during this annual celebration, we are made to realize that we ourselves were slaves in Egypt, and we must have empathy for those who are still in similar straights.

I can't leave the scene of those early Seders at 35 East Jefferson without describing a great divergence that occurred near the beginning of each one. About 15 minutes into the reciting of the *Hagadah*, our great-grandmother, the Bubba Leah, would arrive by taxi and make her presence known by banging her cane on the wooden steps of the porch. On entering the room, she would begin immediately to berate Grandma Noonie for something or other. As mentioned earlier, mother and daughter, had their differences. The fact that the Bubba Leah and her son-in-law, Grandpa Mendel, got along so famously didn't help matters at all, as Mendel would join ranks with Bubba Leah in teasing Noonie.

I, being very young in those early days, had little to add during the service except to mimic my youngest uncle, Alleyboy, who was only six years older. I recall that for a couple of years he would run in and out of the room shouting, "One more hard-boiled egg!" at which all of the adults would laugh and egg him on. To me, it was hilarious, and thinking it was an accepted part of the ceremony, kept it up by way of imitation until I was sent out of the room. There just has to be a fall guy. This anecdote leads me to conclude that while being the oldest grandchild had its benefits, it also had drawbacks. I didn't find out until I was about 14 years old that my middle name wasn't "stupid." It had been my two youngest uncles' mantra.

§

Simchas Torah, commemorating the Jews' receipt of the Torah, is a holiday of singing, dancing, parading and partying. This celebration was right up Grandpa Mendel's and his cronies' alley. After the service in the *shul*, where we youngsters paraded and the elders had a schnaps or two, everyone was invited to 35 East Jefferson for more festivities that would go on quite late. The refreshments consisted of a variety of Eastern European baked goods: *teglach* (round balls of baked dough dipped in honey), *rugelach* (dough rolled with preserves and baked hard), *honelikach* (a delicious honey cake, which in Grandma Noonie's house always had a burnt bottom), strudel (apple being the first choice) and many others. There was, of course, a bottle of whiskey, a bottle of brandy, kosher wine, soft drinks for the kids and tea with lemon and honey.

Far into the night, all the little kids would finally fall asleep on beds, couches and floors, wherever they could lay their little heads. But before conking out, they would make the mess of messes in all the rooms not occupied by the adults. One time, while standing on the bottom drawer to get a peek at a baby asleep in one of the upper drawers, I pulled the highboy chest of drawers over on top of both of us. It was just lucky that the drawers – particularly the top one – opened on the way down and wedged tightly in the guides, giving us just enough space to avoid being crushed.

§

We celebrated not only the Jewish holidays – it seemed the family went into celebration mode whenever there was an excuse to do so. Looking back on those celebrations at my grandparent's house and the *shul*, I'm so happy I was able to enjoy the magic of 35 E. Jefferson and those extended experiences.

PHOTOS:

Me in my holiday suit
My brother Hillard in his suit
(Photographers unknown)

MEL CORREN

The *Shochet* (Ritual Butcher)

Historically, the *shochet* is not only a kosher butcher but he must also be a pious man. In remote communities, the rabbi and the *shochet* can be the same person.

This describes our town *shochet* who also happened to be one of Grandpa Mendel's best friends. Grandpa had many cronies, but "Rabbi" Pinsker stands out in my memory. I don't know if he was actually a rabbi, but he was a kosher butcher - the only one in town - with a good strong singing voice, and he also served as town *mohel* (the ritual circumciser).

"Rabbi" Pinsker could have been type cast for the lead in *Fiddler on the Roof*. He had a big white and slightly reddish beard, a piercing stare and one finger which was cut off at the first knuckle and sprouted what looked to us kids like a small hook – probably the outgrowth of a fingernail. His butcher shop was across the street from the family store and was not exactly

state-of-the-art, so I asked my grandmother one day why she bought her meat from him. Her answer was just as you would have expected from a woman way ahead of her time in terms of understanding and broadmindedness. She told me that the kosher killing of animals for meat had less to do with orderliness and more to do with the way an animal was slaughtered, causing as little pain to it as possible. However, she added, one of the most important aspects of having the *shochet* kill and sell us the meat was because it afforded him the opportunity to earn a living and care for his family.

I believe the main attraction for Grandpa Mendel to this man was his strong bass/baritone voice. They sang all the prayers together, as well as the traditional Yiddish melodies (*nigen*) and songs (*lidlen*). As grandpa and "Rabbi" Pinsker blended their voices, it was as if each attempted to improve on the other's interpretation. They did this not only with their voices, but also with their hands and even fingers, expressing the degree of humor or pathos which each word should convey. They didn't sing for an audience; they sang for themselves.

PHOTO:

The Kosher butcher shop was in this building on Washington Street.(Photographer unknown)

Grandpa and Me

Back to my weekend at Grandpa and Grandma's. If it was early on a Friday or Saturday night when my parents left me off at 35 East Jefferson, I would sit down to dinner at the ample dining room table with bulbous legs and well-worn table pads, the gathering place for everything communal that occurred in the family.

If it was late when I arrived, I would get ready for bed and come to the table. My place was to the left of the seven-branch candelabra and to the right of the ever-present special books – *The Bible*, and *The Writings of the Sages*, which was truly a book of knowledge, containing the condensed stories of all the great men of history until then. Religion, science, literature and other subjects important to civilization are contained in its pages, and its teachings have remained with me for all of these years. Since the articles in this book are all very short, usually not more than a page or two, they are easily read or sat through by a youngster. I see this book as a means of teaching tolerance and the understanding of others to young people, as well as imparting the knowledge and appreciation of the accumulated accomplishments of those who left their marks with the hope of making this a better world.

After the reading and telling of stories, Grandma would make me a cup of her famous hot chocolate, followed by reciting of the *Shema* and *V'ai hoavtah*, the evening prayers.

In the morning, if it was a Saturday (*Shabbat*), Grandpa Mendel and I would go to the Adas Yeshurun *Shul* – the Orthodox synagogue on Fremont Street – where I would sit proudly in the front row with him at my side. We had the privilege of sitting in these seats because Grandpa was one of the leaders of the congregation and the conductor of the choir. After the services we stopped in at M. Corren and Sons, and from there we went out for lunch and a movie.

If it was on a Sunday, we would leave the house and walk or ride the streetcar downtown to Market Street where we would enter the fabulous shop of delightful smells, Muzio's Bakery. There we would load up on snails - not escargot, but the ones with raisins - apple turnovers, cream puffs and Napoleons that have never been equaled.

With our delicacies in hand we would then head to one of the several movie houses located within three or four blocks of one another, sit in Grandpa's favorite section and unwrap and eat our pastries, while being intrigued by the letters, numbers and figures taking their respective turns on the screen as the operator focused the projector.

During this mystical ritual and afterward while watching the movie with Grandpa, I had a feeling of being part of something very special, a fond memory I've enjoyed ever since.

As for the movies themselves, I was totally immersed. If it was a sentimental story, I would cry. If it was a comedy, I would laugh out loud, and if it was scary, I would hide my eyes. However, if it was an action film, I would shake my arms, rise from my seat and grit my teeth. The action movies exhausted me. Certain programs incorporated a vaudeville show between double features – movies shown back-to-back for the single admission price. One time I was treated to a real stage show, a national traveling tour of *The Desert Song*. What a thrill! I hummed and sang the hit song "One Alone" for a long time afterward and, at times, to this day.

Other traveling shows came to town in those days, including musicals featuring young local entertainers who were used as extras to play alongside the headliners. One such company, The O'Neal Sisters, wanted to take my Uncle Izzy – who as a kid was a great song and dance man – along with them, but he was under age. Although I'm sure Grandpa Mendel was on his side, Grandma Noonie wouldn't allow it, and he didn't go.

After the movie, my folks would pick me up in front of the theater, but Grandpa would go on to another one. It mattered not that he might have seen the film before. Grandpa Mendel loved movies. (We grandchildren recently pitched in and bought a seat dedicated to his memory in the renovated Fox California Theatre, renamed the Bob Hope Theatre. (It was Grandpa's favorite and is

now listed on the National register Historical Places.) In those days we had many movie houses in Stockton: The Fox, Sierra, State, the National (which became the Roxy), Ritz, Rialto, The Stockton out north and the Capri in the East. Before my arrival on the scene there were many vaudeville and opera houses that either burned down, converted into movie houses or were destroyed for one reason or another.

Grandpa Mendel's interest in show business went much further than the movies. He loved any form of entertainment. Opera (a singular passion), the symphony, theater, music halls, vaudeville – you name it. In the early days, he traveled by river steamer to San Francisco to attend these events; in later years, he went by train or bus.

Grandpa brought his theatrical passion with him from Russia, where, as previously mentioned, he belonged to an a cappella group of singers and actors. A real bon vivant, he loved a good party, songfest or any other excuse to celebrate with people. He could cook almost anything, including chow mein, but rarely cleaned up the mess.

Grandma, on the other hand, was the anchor of the family, at times to the extreme of not letting any progress disrupt the tried-and-true. She was the one who kept the family close and unified, supplying the glue and strength to endure the everyday obstacles no matter what.

FRIENDS OF THE FOX

242 E. MAIN STREET • STOCKTON, CALIFORNIA 95202
(209) 462-2692 (209) 462-2783 FAX

July 25, 2005

Mr. Mel Corren
6851 Gettysburg Place
Stockton CA 95207

Dear Mr. Corren:

On behalf of the Friends of the Fox, I thank you for your April 20, 2005 donation of $ 250 to participate in the Fox Theatre "Save My Seat" campaign.   The seat that you selected to honor Mendel Corren will have a plaque inscribed as follows:

Mendel Corren
Love, His Grandchildren

PHOTOS:

Grandpa Mendel

Me

Uncle Izzy

(Unknown photographers)

J. D. Peters, the steamer Grandpa Mendel probably took to San Francisco (Photo courtesy of University of the Pacific archives, Holt Atherton Special Collection)

Acknowledgment from Friends of the Fox on the purchase of a commemorative seat

The Third Generation

I had an older sister who died shortly after birth because she couldn't digest our mother's milk. They tried to feed her with evaporated milk, but she couldn't digest that either. Today she may have survived with lactose and dairy substitutes, but that was then. She is buried in the Ahavas Aachim cemetery along with so many others of our family. So, with my birth, I became the oldest member of the third generation.

We lived on Ophir Street in an apartment across the hall from our cousins, Al and Ann Metzger and their children, Ethel and Leland. Ethel and Leland were not only our cousins, but our lifelong best friends as well. We seemed always to live close to one another.

We moved from the apartment on Ophir to a little house on Ash Court, a cul de sac at the East end of Alder Street which has since been renamed as a continuation of that street.

The Harry Correns then moved to a house one block west of ours, and our two families in some ways became an extension of each other's. To Noonie's dismay, both families then began living a little more independently from Mendel and Noo–nie who lived on the south side of town.

It was here, three and a half years after me, that my brother, Hillard, was born. Being a boy, he was a traumatic shock to our mother, Goldie, who had hoped to have a daughter to replace the one she lost.

As a result of this disappointment, Mother developed a postpartum depression which took a salt water treatment at the Santa Cruz beach to cure.

The Gianellis lived across the street and had two daughters and a son. I remember playing out in front of the house with Louise, one of the sisters my age, and we have remained friends – along with one of her daughters – these many years.

The Briones family lived next door. Mr. Briones was the boy's department manager of the at the Stockton Dry Goods Department Store on Main and American Streets. They had a daughter and two sons who were older than me. Their daughter sometimes babysat with me, and during WWII, Uncle Al and I met one of their sons, Elwyn, in London. We were walking along Oxford Street, and there he was walking toward us. It was quite a surprise, as can be imagined, to meet a former neighbor in a place so far away.

Uncle Harry and Auntie Esther were married just about the same time I was born in 1924. Esther was from Donkera in Latvia, and came to America on a first-class ticket. Her older brothers, Max and Manuel Cohen, were both doing well here and had sent for her. She was born into and grew up in a very poor environment but, as a result of this passage, developed an appetite for only the best.

When Uncle Harry met and married the "new kid on the block," there began a love affair which lasted more than 50 years.

Uncle Harry and Auntie Esther lived one block west of us on Alder Street in a house with a big front porch, and they had a son and daughter, Irving and Marilyn. Living with them were Esther's parents, Helman and Tirtza Cohen. Helman had a long black-and-gray wiry beard with a tobacco stain all around the lips. Although he came to America, he went on living in the same exact way as he had in the old country only with better sanitation and other amenities. He walked to *shul*, *davened* (prayed all the daily prayers), and drank steaming hot soup and tea.

Irv's Grandpa Helman had, besides a passion for cigarettes and food, a love affair with wrestling and fast cars. He would love to go to the wrestling matches and shout encouragement to his favorite wrestler in Yiddish, and while riding in the car with Harry, he would holler, *"Gicher, Gicher!* (Faster, Faster!)"* while leaning over Harry with his hands on the steering wheel.

Irv's Grandma Tirtza was a great cook and baker, but was very suspicious of strangers. She often cautioned Irv and Marilyn in a singsong voice, *"Sahg gorneisht* (Say nothing),"* when they were entertaining their friends. I suppose it was a bit of paranoia left over from the old country.

In about 1930 or so, the Harry Corren family moved across the street from our family on West Walnut Street. Harry and Dad continued to work in the furniture store for their father. It wasn't a get-rich-quick kind of job, so they teamed up to live better. They shared one car between families. First, a big 1930 Buick and then a couple of Chevys until each family was able to afford its own car some years later. A fond memory of my childhood was the six of us, including some of my uncles, coming home in one car from the family store, and making the inevitable stop at Muzio's bakery just a block from the store to get a loaf of French bread or half a dozen hard rolls. This was at the behest of Auntie Esther who had called Harry just before takeoff. The loaf of French bread never made it home in one piece because everyone in the car broke a little off the end to nosh on. As you can imagine, much of the bread arrived D.O.A.

Speaking of the cars, a famous story has it that on one hot summer Sunday, we all – the Harry and the Sam Correns – piled into the car they owned together and headed out to Yosemite National Park for the day. We were not only stuffed into the car, but along with us was a large picnic lunch. While winding around the hills, Irving, who had a slightly delicate stomach, complained that he was getting a bit queasy, so we stopped for a minute to let him give back a little breakfast. A few miles later, I began to complain that I was getting nauseated; however, my mother dismissed my pleas to stop, convinced I was only copying Irving. It wasn't long before we did have to stop. Yes, we stopped and washed off the covering of the lunch and some of our clothing as well. We did get to Yosemite all right, but this unscheduled stop put a bit of a damper on the trip as you can well imagine. Mother never lived it down, and it was always a topic of conversation when we played "Remember When?"

There was a special relationship between my mother and auntie Esther who were the first two to have taken sons away from Grandma Noonie. This special relationship often became a downright heavy one because they were both good homemakers, cooks and bakers. The competition was often quite fierce. They entertained beautifully, but Goldie could never top Esther's chocolate layer cake, nor Esther, Goldie's strudel. Goldie also prevailed with her kosher pickles, the "snap" of which became family legend.

In later years this recipe would play a part in the wonderful friendship we enjoyed with our friends Arnold and Becca Sheuerman and Keith and Peggy Cornell, with whom we put up pickles and had wonderful times. Becca, Peggy and Harriet prepared the ingredients, Keith procured the materials, Dr. Arnold oversaw the sterility aspects and I was in charge of determining the proper salt content.

There were the specialties: Auntie Esther made *parogan* like none other (a special, delicious meat loaf mix, wrapped in a bread-like dough and baked brown to perfection. It's traditional name is *pierogy*, but she called it *parogan*). Then there was the *cioppino* created of fish and shellfish that Goldie made from a recipe handed down to her from her father-in-law, Mendel.

This *cioppino* recipe was enhanced by Ma Busalacchi, the matriarch of a grand old Italian family that had the fish business sewed up in Stockton. Ma often hosted an open house in her basement - almost every Italian family had a basement with a completely equipped kitchen, dining table and a couple of easy chairs. It was a special treat to be invited to her house for a meal.

You could count on a delicious minestrone, chicken (fried or roasted), baccala or polenta and always plenty of spaghetti and ravioli. What a special woman, and what a special family!

My dad was crazy about Ma, and I know it was mutual. Every time Dad had a cold or bursitis, Ma had a home-style cure – a thick sweet wine for coughs and cactus juice or poultices for various aches and pains.

While living on Walnut Street, I attained my greatest success as a pianist. My cousin Irv and I began taking piano lessons from Joe Mello on the same day in a little place on Market Street, upstairs and across the street from the barber shop. Grandpa Mendel had sold the Mellos some furniture and accepted payment as piano lessons for the two of us. I began like a house on fire, having been assigned my first piece of discernible music, a simplified version of "La Dona Mobile" from Verdi's *Rigoletto*. I had arrived. I was a pianist. Irv received his first piece of music the same day – a little song called "Bluebirds." I've always maintained that the fact that he received that mundane little tune spurred him on to greatness. It was as if he wasn't going to take that insult without response, and his response was to pursue his study of the piano the way he pursued everything else he took on in life: diligently. Irv became a very accomplished musician, playing in dance bands, and ultimately leading his own. He played as a guest artist with the Stockton Symphony Orchestra and enjoyed the fruits of popularity because of his ability to play the piano so well.

However, he came home from the war and studied law because, as he told me, while overseas he was able to attend a music school sponsored by the army at which Dave Brubeck was also studying, and after hearing Dave, he decided to change his focus.

After my brief brush with operatic success, it was all down hill for me. I did not succumb to the practice of practicing the piano. Because Mr. Mello thought I had a good touch, he gave me lessons for many years. All the while, my mother kept telling me that if I would learn to play, I could be the life of the party. Instead, I have had to rely on blarney.

By the way, Mr. Mello didn't owe grandpa so much money that he continued to give our lessons in payment for the entire time we studied with him. At one point the folks had to begin paying him $1.50 per half hour for the weekly lesson.

My personal reward for my labors at the piano came when we took our lessons in the Chinese restaurant/nightclub on Weber Avenue called The Golden Dragon. There was a mystique about being up there on that little stage, even though the restaurant was empty. It really stirred my imagination, but I must again admit that the chicken noodle soup was my greatest incentive. Joe taught us during the day when the restaurant was closed, and the staff brought us food and fortune cookies. He was long-suffering, and told my mother repeatedly about my good touch.

I was recently at a birthday party for my sister-in law in San Jose, where a Chinese man was seated at our table. When he found out we were from Stockton, he told us he was as well, adding that his father had owned a Chinese night club and restaurant there. It turned out to be the same Golden Dragon where my cousin, Irv., learned to play the piano and I enjoyed the noodle soup. When I told him about those days in the 1930s., he remembered our teacher, Joe Mello.

I and all my friends had birthday parties which were really super. Each mother would create a special luncheon, ostensibly for the children, but more likely as a kind of one-upmanship. They would set the table as if for an adult dinner party, although the decorations were geared to a child's birthday. Each setting had several pieces of silver and separate plates for each course, with meals served to suit a gourmet. We children reacted to all of this as one would expect: We shot peas at one another across the table with dinner knives as the propelling tools. We ran around the table tweaking each others' ears and generally causing a ruckus, while being very careful not to eat any of the special food that had been prepared to have room for the birthday cake and ice cream.

After the meal and the opening of the presents – books, games, balls and the like (no clothes at these parties) – we were carted off downtown to a movie. This affair was called a Theater Party. It was due to one of these – the party planned for my brother Hillard's seventh birthday – that I suffered one of my earliest disappointments. I awoke that morning, May 11, 1934, anticipating a grand day of feasting and film, when I heard the news that my mother was in the hospital. She had given birth to my sister, Doralee, seven years to the day after

Hillard. To say I was disappointed would be stating it mildly, but I soon came to terms. Doralee has not only been a great sister to me but also to my wife, Harriet, who regards her as the sister she never had. Although we're from the same family, Doralee, who is 10 years younger, always reminds me that we were raised in different households. I grew up during the Depression, while she lived in a family that could support her Spalding/cashmere lifestyle.

Hillard did well in school and was always the peacemaker in our home. Whenever (usually) I was in trouble with Mom, he would come to my rescue. Once, for instance, when it was my turn to wash the dishes, I experimented to see how high I could make the suds rise in the sink. He assuaged our mother's anger by suggesting I go out to the can (that is, to play "Kick the Can") while he finished doing the dishes.

During WWII, Hillard joined the Navy and was stationed at Treasure Island. When he returned home, he decided to begin working with Uncle Alleyboy in the appliance store. It was lucky for us that he learned there how to take care of the business end, as that ability made us successful in The Brothers as well as in our retirements.

Cousin Marilyn was the bridge between the Harry and Sam families and was like another sister to Hillard and me. At an early age she developed the attitude that everything belonged to her. Hence her nickname "Minee," bestowed upon her by Uncle Izzy. He adored her, fawned over her, and bought her presents, so when he married Auntie Vera, it was quite a trauma for her.

We – Mel, Hillard and Irving – as well as our sisters, Marilyn and Doralee, grew up more like siblings than cousins. Elaine and Bernard were Auntie Sadie and Uncle Ernest's children. They lived in San Francisco on the same block as Harriet, and years later Elaine would introduce me to her.

Arnold was Auntie Rosie and Uncle Dan's only son. He sometimes lived in San Francisco and other times in Stockton and Los Angeles. Mike and Evelyn had two children: Suzanne, the female cousin closest to Doralee's age, making them close friends; and a younger son, Craig, who is an attorney.

Leonard was Maurice and Sophie's only child. He lived in Stockton, the Bay Area, Santa Cruz and Oregon. and was a respected professor at Delta College before becoming a family counselor.

Charlyne and Barbara Lee are Izzy and Vera's daughters and live in Las Vegas and San Jose.

Mendelle and Patricia are Allen and Gertrude's daughters and live in Stockton and Los Angeles.

We cousins are in different age brackets, making those closest in age closer to one another, but in our adult years we have grown very close.

PHOTOS:

Auntie Esther with Tirtza, her mother
My sister, Doralee
Hillard, me, Irv and Marilyn on an outing

Growing Up In Stockton

Ours was a great neighborhood, and we kids had marvelous times together.

Our best times were spent doing simple things like riding our bikes around the neighborhood, going to Scout meetings and outings, participating in school sports and playing games such as Kick the Can or pitching pennies – when we could get them – and many other no-cost recreations. Sitting around shooting the breeze was the way we showed off our acquired knowledge of the many things that interest young boys. In those early years, girls were with girls and boys with boys until they happened onto the common denominator.

We each went Snipe Hunting only one time. Snipe hunting is/was a prank played on naive youngsters that called for a burlap bag and a stick. When the novice was sent out into the field alone, he was instructed to make a call to attract the snipe. All the other kids would leave, and soon the victim would realize he'd been had.

Bob Fleming, who lived next door to me, was not only a neighbor but a good friend. His claim to fame was that he was a very good tennis player and played on the high school team. One Sunday his parents invited me to go on a picnic at Oak Park and they had sweet pickles, which I had never before tasted – kosher pickles were the only ones we ever had at home. I ate so many that I was sick to my stomach for two days. I ate the next one about 60 years later.

Bob and I were very creative in high school. An example: He was the president of the "Block S Society", the athletes' club, and appointed me as his assistant in organizing a dance, even though I wasn't a member. We were excused from school to get the necessary items for decorations, but spent most of the afternoon just goofing off. To provide an excuse for our absence, we went to my family's furniture store and made a phonograph record on a new invention, the Recordio, a precursor of tape recorders. On that record we recited and sang a little ditty we made up as an excuse for our absence and gave it to the attendance monitor, Miss Robbins. She was a tough attendance monitor but she

excused us because she had never received such an original excuse in her many years "on the bench".

We lived two houses east of the Dean De Carli family. Dean was a dairy man who later became mayor of the city, the founder of Stockton's sister city, and a renowned civic leader. De Carli Plaza, a large public square at the Downtown Stockton Waterfront, was named for him. The children in the De Carli family – Dolores, Joan and Gail – were younger than me, however, Dolores, is a good friend of my sister Doralee's, and Harriet and I have remained friends with Joan De Carli, now Cortopassi, and her husband, Dino.

Marlene Below, now Hnath, was also born on that famous street and being about 10 years younger than me is a lifelong friend of my sister, Doralee. However, that isn't her only relevance to this tome, because as you might recall, she was the one who reconnected me with my army buddy, Bob Rieders, and recently, along with my friend Barbra Schwartz, played a prominent role in my having been named "Stocktonian of the Year 2015.".

I had my bar mitzvah while living on Walnut Street, as did my cousin Irv. Both events drew big crowds along with many gifts, which in those days tended to be hair brush sets, books, neckties and the ever popular fountain pen. A current joke at the time was that the bar mitzvah boy would say in his speech that he thanked everyone for his or her gift, especially the one who gave him a fountain pen. "It should leak from his nose as it does from that pen." I, like many of us kids, sold subscriptions and delivered magazines on a weekly basis. I sold *Saturday Evening Post, Ladies Home Journal* and *Country Gentleman.* I worked for Mr. Scantelbury, and enjoyed the most regular regimen of exercising I've ever had by climbing up and down all twelve flights of stairs in the Medical Dental Building once a week. Irv sold *Liberty,* and we would compare our products and discuss who had the best route.

A special event each fall was the crushing of the grapes in Irv's family's driveway. It was a messy job, done under the watchful direction of Irv's Grandpa Hellman, since it was strictly kosher.

Other memorable events included tasting the *lokshn* (noodle soup) made by Irv's Grandma Tirtza for her husband. She served it to him piping hot every Friday night in a large mixing bowl. It was fun to watch him slurp it through his cigarette-stained beard from a huge silver spoon. We children thought the spoon had been made for a giant. It is now a framed reminder of times past and hangs on a wall in Irv's son Marc's house.

Can you imagine being a youngster (about 10 years old) and living next door to an Olympic boxing champion? Well, I did. Our neighbor to the East, Fred Feary, won that honor, and we all felt a part of it. His younger cousin, Doug Ross, who lived with Fred's family, was my age, so I got to go over to their house to visit. Fred later became a policeman and then a news photographer. He married Edith and they had a daughter, Coraleta, who has remained a good friend of ours.

I looked forward to helping decorate the Christmas tree at the Ross' house, since I could not have one at home. I think it was even more exciting for me than it was for the Ross family. It was great fun, and the refreshments were good as well.

In the evening, we played Tag and Kick the Can seemingly for hours on the corner in front of Irv's house to the strains of his piano practicing.

We even had snow one day in Stockton, while living on Walnut Street, and went outside to get our fill of this new phenomenon.

What a thrill it was the first time I was allowed to ride my bicycle down to Yosemite Lake, about four blocks away. It is now called Legion Park and is not as frequently used as before. It was a special treat to go to the lake during the week, but on the Fourth of July, when the fireworks were set off there, it was extra special – a genuine happening. The lake is at the base of a grass-covered levee, which on the Fourth was covered with blankets, pets and families.

Swimming was allowed there in those days, and the undertow accounted for occasional drownings, mostly youngsters. There were other sad times as well, such as the night Irv's Grandpa Hellman, after lighting a cigarette in its long holder and placing it in an ashtray on the mantle, left the room for a moment and died suddenly. It seemed eerie that the cigarette continued to burn after his life had been extinguished.

I also did my share of packing up a little sack and running away from home when things didn't go my way but since it always seemed to be evening when I got the urge, I would turn back when I arrived at the foreboding empty lot at the corner of Walnut and Pacific. Then, all the way home I would invent reasons why I decided to return and forgive everyone concerned. I think the reason it was so fashionable then for youngsters to run away from home was due to the literature and movies of the time which featured that behavior as a response to trouble at home.

While my mother shopped in the Piggly Wiggly grocery store, Johnny, the butcher, would often give me a free "weeney" to munch, but one time I carried the free idea a little too far. When we arrived home, mother caught sight of the candy bar I had pinched, and made me go back to the grocer and fess up. A great and lasting lesson.

Mother's mother, Grandma Dora, who was a jewel, died while we lived on Walnut Street. It was the same day the canary flew out of its cage and was never seen again. Grandpa Mendel, who was not only the patriarch of our immediate family, but to many other families in the community as well, also died while we lived on Walnut, and was lamented by all.

He was a man who believed in the goodness of man, and lived his life trying to prove it. He came to this country with two dollars in his pocket and a desire to better himself and his family as Americans. His love for the theater and all things musical and theatrical must have come down to him from his father, a *Chazan* (Cantor).

I was about twelve when my lifelong friend Geri Miller Berkman became my first date. She invited me to a Halloween party given by her girl friend. The party was an eye-opener for a 12-year-old boy, what with bobbing for apples and that new sport – for me, at least – that entailed spinning the bottle to get a kiss from one of the girls. I suppose this was my introduction to the big game of Boy seeks Girl. It kind of set me up for the next game I discovered in later years, strip poker. Of all the games I ever played, not one of them lasted long enough.

Incidentally, another first occurred that night: At midnight, Jackie's father took us all a few blocks down to Victory Park, where at the entrance stood an authentic Totem Pole (it has recently been removed as a result of old age), and told us scary stories in keeping with Halloween. I had never before been out that late without my parents.

§

We grew up in the heart of the Depression, but fortunately for us, we didn't feel it as much as many families who were really suffering. I do, however, remember on one occasions when I had a hole in my shoe, my mother showed me how to cover it with a couple of playing cards to keep my foot from touching the ground.

Cousin Lee Metzger was an all-around athlete in grammar school and received the Athlete of the Year Award at an assembly just before he contracted an illness which put him to bed for a whole semester. It was a rare condition and never diagnosed, but it exempted him from the draft. Today they would have a name for it and possibly a cure, but in those days they attributed it to a severe growing reaction. He had always been the smallest of us, but he suddenly shot to his adult height of 6'4" or so in a very short time.

Charles Metzger, Leland's grandfather, was a brewer who made beer in the basement of the house on Lomita Avenue and had an aviary in the back yard. Years later, when Lee and his son Keith came to Stockton to make a movie of his life, Lee bet me that there wasn't a basement in that house. Since Leland always won, I didn't bet, but it could have been the first time he lost. He asked the person who now lived there and found out that not only was there a basement, but the current owner also put up beer in it.

We played Monopoly for hours at Lee's house, and he would end up with all the hotels and houses. He was a born business man with a photographic memory, which he used to great advantage at the card table. He bet on anything and could have made a living playing gin. Maybe he did.

Next door to the Metzgers lived a couple of bachelors who were great adventurers. One of them brought home a huge lizard he had had preserved and donated to the local Haggin Museum. We kids often rode our bikes to the museum to view the beast and brag that we knew the man who had bagged it.

Being a part of a large and extended family was a wild and wonderful experience. It was not uncommon to meet someone on the street who would inquire about a member of the family.

When I picked up the telephone receiver to make a call, a real live operator would ask, "Number please?" When I answered with the telephone number of the store, 1141, the operator would sometimes ask, "Which one is your father?" If I had a conversation with someone new to me, I could always identify myself by mentioning a close or distant relative, whom the person almost certainly either knew or knew of.

When I was very young I din't feel comfortable meeting new adults until one night when I was about 10 years old. My dad took me to a B'nai Brith or Eagles meeting (I can't remember which) and preceded me into the crowded hall. As I stood at the double doors, I froze for a moment, and then, all of a sudden, it struck me that if ever I was going to get over my shyness with adults, it was at that moment. I girded my loins and, while firmly shaking the hand of each adult, made a brief remark. It was a wonderful new experience and I haven't stopped greeting and talking since.

When I meet youngsters about ten years old I shake hands with them and receive jellyfish shakes in return. I then squeeze more firmly and tell them when you shake another person's hand you want that person to know you are really interested by really squeezing. This I demonstrate somewhat exaggeratedly and years later, when they return from college, I get a very firm shake with knowing eye contact. It makes my day.

We were also Boy Scouts and had the distinction of being members of Troop one. We met in the Methodist church where we learned to tie knots and accomplish the various other activities necessary to win the coveted Merit Badges which, when a scout has earned a minimum of 21, makes him eligible to become an Eagle Scout, the most prestigious rank in the organization

It seemed like all the Boy Scout Camporees (overnights in various parks) were the same. We

had fun practicing for our badges, but it seemed there was always sand in the food we prepared. The only one of us who became an Eagle Scout was Jack Stillman, who, incidentally was the first person who I ever knew to have a ruptured appendix.

Stockton was a small town with just a touch of sophistication, and if this paints a picture of Stockton as an idyllic place in which to grow up and live, it surely was that, and more.

PHOTOS:

Gene Cohen, Leland Metzger, Irving, me, Tom Hogan, Bob Flemming
Bob Flemming and me
Plaque at De Carli Plaza
Fred Feary Bronze winner of Olympics 1932 for boxing. (courtesy of Coraleta Faery Rogers)
Snow in Stockton! – Hillard, Mom and me
Geri Troop One. Boy Scouts of America (Photographer unknown)

Early Schooling

My earliest memories of school life was the day my mother took me for a walk to our new home on Walnut Street. We were crossing the street en route to our newly rented home when my mother told me that the school was just behind our house, and that I could walk there. To this day I remember the excitement the prospect of going to school aroused in me.

Kindergarten was a time of discovery until I found that my humor frequently caused me to be sent to the place of detention, which was under the elevated sand box. Thus began a round robin of like behavior and punishment. My fellow students would break up and I suppose I did it to attract attention, but as a result my teachers must have passed along my reputation since it seemed that although I would often know the answer, I was rarely called upon. I would almost wear out my arm – to no avail. I can only guess they feared if they called on me I might come up with something disruptive.

In grammar school I enjoyed Washington Irving's tales of the Catskill Mountains. Many years later, when our son Donald moved to an area near the Catskills, I was transported back in time to those days in my eighth grade classroom.

I enjoyed the social aspects of schooling to a fault, but studying was another thing. I didn't conquer my inertia until I began doing things that really challenged and excited me. These tasks made me oblivious of time and soon I recognized that I enjoyed coloring and putting things together. As a result, I enjoyed going to the family furniture store to help dress the windows, hang draperies and create room settings. I could spend hours until the work I was doing pleased me, no matter how long it took or how many times I had to redo a troublesome detail. It followed, therefore, that I would be attracted to interior decorating as a vocation, which would not only be fulfilling, but would also provide a good living for my family.

I found that looking at a project, coming up with a plan, selling that plan, putting it into action, and then, on the day of reckoning, setting it up in the house, was so exciting that I often marveled that I could actually earn money doing which gave me so much pleasure. The remuneration was always secondary, although it just kept coming.

I once decorated a home for a psychologist who, observing how happy I was while arranging the furniture and hanging the wall decor, asked me how I felt when I was doing these things. I remember telling him that it all started with the plan, selling the plan, ordering the furnishings – including the furniture, draperies and wall decor – then, when it all arrived, loading, delivering and setting it up. I "blew him away" when I told him that when I'm in the home and assembling the pieces into a whole, I feel like a symphony conductor whose job it is to wave his wand and bring all the wonderful sounds together.

I have a great memory of walking through the big empty lot which connected the school to our house and petting Mr. Molini's horse. He was, I think, a he, and so big that I was really scared at first.

Although we lived behind the school, I was very often late for the opening bell. It seems there was always something that had to be done at the last minute, and that hasn't changed much to this day.

At El Dorado School, I played baseball as the pitcher, while my cousin Al Davidson did the catching, but I had to stop when, at practice, I threw an inside pitch which almost did him in.

I also tried my foot as a place kicker in football. I dreamed up the idea of the toe cap and ball holder before they were ever used. I took an old rubber galosh and cut out everything but the heel and toe, leaving the sides on to hold them together for the cap, and used a cup-shaped stand for the holder. It worked quite well, but the coach was negative about the idea. Since then I've eaten my heart out every time I've watched a kicker use what might have been my proverbial "Safety Pin" invention.

I tried skiing. Once!

An outstanding sports event which Irv and I would bring up when talking about old "El Deeero," is the football game we played against Manual Training School, which fielded a team made up of huge, really tough guys. We trained for two weeks or so for that game, which was played at the Armory, across from the old Stockton High School. We even improvised protective gear so they wouldn't kill us, but they did anyway – figuratively, of course.

I played a little tennis but my career was cut short when I played a game with my niece. Although I was trounced, I managed to develop a nasty case of bursitis. which caused me to give up the game.

I was told by some cracker jack business men that I would make more sales on the golf course than in the store. but on my first outing when I was on the third tee ready to drive that long one, I happened to look over my shoulder and noticed I could no longer see the club house.

I then figured that the ninth hole was even further away, making me wonder what I was doing out there communing with nature when I should have been working.

I can say, however, that competitive sports were never my cup of tea.

My dad was very serious regarding the furniture business and subscribed to various industry periodicals. One day he brought home a booklet, which I still have, written by Ross Crane, who, in 1928, was considered a foremost authority on interior decorating (a paragraph in this 1920s book states that linoleum has come into its own).

The Seng Spring Company, which manufactured springs for the furniture industry, occasionally printed a booklet of this type and distributed it to retailers to make furniture salespeople aware of new trends. The Ross Crane edition discussed the interior decorating service that general furniture stores would soon be

offering to their customers (before that decorators were only available to the wealthy) and emphasized that the well-being of occupants would be greatly affected by the orientation of the house and its furnishings. This impressed me so much that when my counselor, during the first week of high school, asked what I wanted to do with my life, I told her I wanted to be a psychological interior decorator. I gave that answer because I felt that Mr. Crane, in his book, was presenting interior decoration in a new light, approaching it from the standpoint of meeting the aesthetic as well as the psychological needs of the customer/client. My counselor just smiled the only smile I ever saw on her face for the next four years, and said in her strange little voice, "If you do half as well as your uncle Allen, maybe we can get you into college."

Starting high school is a new and trying experience but added to that, in my case, was the fact that I tended to stoop. My father, who always admonished me to stand up straight, brought home a "treasure," which at the time I abhorred but which proved to be one of the best "gifts" I've ever received. It was a harness for me to wear under my shirt which forced my shoulders back, thereby causing me to walk without stooping. It was not only physically painful, but it added to the stress I was going through, since I had to dress and undress in front of all my fellow "athletes" during gym periods.

Since my father had sung "La Dona Mobile" in Professor Flavio Flavius's *a cappella* group, I decided to take Italian for my high school language requirement. Except for me and one other student, the class I joined consisted of Italian-American kids who already spoke Italian and were interested in an easy grade. I made great friends, and the teacher, Mr. Vannuccini, was wonderful. We had an Italian club, went out to Italian dinners and generally got into the Italian thing, but shortly after my second year, war with Italy broke out and they cancelled the class. All of

us in class were devastated and I never again saw Mr. Vannuccini, although, I've retained fond memories of him. I was transferred to a Spanish class, but could never get into that language as I had in Italian. However, while in France during World War II, I learned to speak French, if not perfectly, at least tolerably.

In my opinion, the discontinuance of the German and Italian language classes was a foolish move. It would have been wiser to have added to them, following the example set by the U.S. Army, which opened language schools teaching German and Italian, languages, i.e., the Language School in Monterey, California.

While I was in high school, Uncle Al married Aunt Gertrude and since they were not much older than me, I thought of them as just friends. I would walk over to their duplex, about three blocks from the school, and spend my lunch hour with them. I'd visit with Gert until Al came home for lunch, then stay on with the two of them until I had to go back to school. In later years I could only imagine their annoyance with me for taking up their whole "lunch hour". Had I not done that, their oldest child, Mendelle, could possibly be a little older.

PHOTOS:

El Dorado School photo of third grade, Miss Fitch. (Brownel Studios, Stockton, Unavailable)
Ski Bum
My dad showing early linoleum (Photographer: Ernest Stenciled Co. 765 Market St. S.F. (Unavailable)
Me before the brace (Logan Studios, Stockton unavailable)
El Dorado Grammar School graduating class of January. 1938. School photo. (Photographer unknown)

Religious Schooling

We attended *chaider* every weekday after grammar school, as well as Sunday School, at the Jewish Community Center on the corner of Willow and Madison streets. These two handsome buildings were the pride of the Stockton Jewish Community until the 1960s, when the temple, left facing, was declared a hazard and razed. (the core of this building was the earliest temple building, moved from its original site and refaced to match the new building alongside).

A new temple was then built at its present El Dorado Street location and the above Community Center building became a storage annex for the Stockton Civic Theatre and later a home for low-income senior citizens which it remains today.

In *chaider* one day I heard that a classmate drowned at the old Olympic Baths on the South side of town. He was the first of our group to die and it seemed eerie to me that he had sat next to me just a few days before.

We played wonderful football and baseball games in the yard of the church across from the temple when we were supposed to be in class. The various *malamadim* (teachers of Hebrew and Judaism) used different approaches to get us back into the classroom.

The Hebrew teacher I remember best is the one who would grab your hand, bend one

MAURICE COHEN *GENEVIEVE SCHWARTZ* *JOE SCHWARTZ* *SID ROSEN* *DR WALLER POS* *1224 COHEN* *MEL COHEN/REUBEN PORES* *BEN PORES* *MORT UNGEN* *JAKE KRAMASKY* *GOLDBERG* *BOBBY MILLER* *ALVIN DAVIDSON* *LELAND METZGER* *ETHYL METZGER*

PURIM SHPIEL CIRCA -1938
TEMPLE ISRAEL ON MADISON ST.
(JEWISH COMMUNITY CENTER)

finger backward in a submission hold, and lead you back to class as you twisted and turned to free yourself from his grip.

Benny Pores and I were guards in an all-Yiddish speaking Purim play that the Hebrew school staged. In the play, Benny tells me, in Yiddish, that he overheard a plot to kill the king, and I answer: "*Shvieg Shtil de venten habbin everen*" ("Be quiet! The walls have ears!")

Now at 92 plus, I look forward to reprising those lines in the next Purim *shpiels* at the reform temple. Nowadays, though, the words have to be translated by the next speaker.

Would you believe that on Passover, when we had matzos in our school lunch, and on other Jewish holidays, we had excuses to stay out of school, some of our schoolmates wanted to be Jewish?

PHOTOS:

Temple Israel (now razed) and the Jewish Community Center which is now a home for low-income seniors (Photographer unknown).

An all Yiddish speaking Purim play in the Jewish Community Center (Performers from Adas Yeshurun Chaider) Circa 1940

Troop One Boy Scouts of America, Stockton, Ca.

(Photographers unknown)

MEL CORREN

Early Travels

We looked forward to Summer because school was out and we could do many fun things. The family went on vacation, either to visit relatives out of town or to explore places of interest.

When we kids were young, the Sam and Harry Corren families vacationed in the Santa Cruz area. Sometimes we stayed at a hotel across from the Boardwalk; other times we stayed at the Happy Valley Resort in the mountains just above the town. Benny Pores's family also stayed there, and we really had a ball.

There was a bowling alley with two lanes, and one of the older kids served as pin

setter. It was usually Benny's brother, Leonard. We rode all the rides on the Boardwalk and waded in the ocean, and, when we were a little older, we went fishing off the pier. I remember catching a fairly large fish one time, and my dad had the chef at the hotel prepare it for dinner. Boy, did I feel special.

Dad enjoyed driving, so sometimes we went to far-off places. One year we drove across country all the way to Duluth, Minnesota, where mother's family greeted us like long-lost cousins, which we were. Minnesota was beautiful, interesting and loaded with mosquitos. We stayed with Aunt Annie's family in Duluth while Dad went on to Chicago to attend his first big Furniture Market at The Merchandise Mart in the Windy City. The Mart was the largest building in the country and the capitol of the furniture industry in 1937.

Another wonderful trip was to Vancouver. It didn't start out that way, because when we stopped to say goodbye to Uncle Ernest and Auntie Sadie in San Francisco, our car was broken into and everything stolen. We had to buy new clothing for the trip as well as new luggage. Hillard and I thought it fun, but the folks were, quite naturally, a little perturbed. That wasn't the end of our misfortune either, because when we arrived in Seattle, we were informed by Uncle Harry and Auntie Esther, who were watching over our dog, Muggins, that she had been dognapped. Now it was Hillard's and my turn to be upset. We decided we were going right back home, but we were overruled. Muggins was never found, but as the days passed we focused more on the trip's adventures and less on our loss. When we came home it didn't seem the same without her, so dad got us another Boston terrier, a male we named Skippy. He was a feisty little guy and, as a result, went through life with one eye.

You've already read about the ill-fated trip to Yosemite in the crowded car plus lunch, but we continued to go on other mountain rides. We spent a week or two almost every summer at Lake Tahoe. We stayed on the South side near the state line at a very comfortable motel that consisted of a series of cabins. Every year, the owners would try to sell my dad on the idea of investing in the property for either renting or developing. My dad kept refusing even though the price was right, but there came a time when the offer was no longer on the table. The road next to the property became either a ski run or a ski lift for the Heavenly Valley Olympics of 1960. This turned Heavenly Valley into one of the finest ski resorts in the country. That's how fortunes are made and lost in the wink of an eye.

We visited relatives in Los Angeles from time to time, and the biggest thrill was going to the famous restaurants on La Cienega Boulevard, where I was always on the lookout but never saw a movie star. Many years later on a trip to London, Harriet and I visited her famous cousin, Walter Shenson, a movie producer (google him). He took us in his Rolls Royce Cornish convertible to the exclusive White Elephant Club, where I sat back to back with Charlie Chaplin and his wife, Oona.

Who could forget the good times we had in Ocean Park, California, where Auntie Schiffera lived right on the beach and where Grandpa Mendel loved to spend part of the summer?

Our family sometimes vacationed there at the same time as my cousin Alvin Davidson's did and along with swimming and sand castles we

again gave the rides and amusements on the Boardwalk a workout.

Alas, however, it was too early in life for Alvin and me to be interested in the real sights as they displayed themselves on the beach.

The Correns were always well represented at the twice-yearly Furniture Markets in San Francisco and Los Angeles. and we stayed in fine hotels. During the day, Dad shopped for merchandise and at night we ate in fine restaurants when there wasn't a doings of some kind connected with the Furniture Association.

In later years when Hillard and I had the Brothers Interior Furnishings, we made use of this early training, but expanded upon it by going to

markets and furniture factories in High Point, NC, Dallas, Atlanta, Paris, Milan, Brussels, and Beijing. At those events we traded ideas with friends in the furniture business from far and near.

Once, on a buying trip to the Paris Market, Harriet and I took time out to visit the Louvre.

As we approached the *Venus De Milo*, we heard, "Hey, Mel!" It was one of the road salesmen who regularly called on our store.

In those days, almost all the members of the furniture industry, from the smallest retail stores to the largest factories, were family owned and operated. The buyers representing the retail stores and the sellers representing the factories were a very close-knit group and when we attended the showrooms at the semiannual Furniture Markets in San Francisco and Los Angeles, where the new styles were being presented, we were treated to buffets at lunchtime, snacks in the afternoon and cocktails in the evening. It was a very convivial relationship. When we were together at industry events you wouldn't have guessed that we were competitors... that is, as I knew it to be with the furniture dealers in Stockton.

Mrs. Henry Ullman, along with her husband and son were, along with many others too numerous to mention, good friends as well as business associates. With some we continued a relationship even after we were no longer in business.

We didn't travel only for business. We made it a point to take time off during the year to visit other interesting places as well.

As has already been mentioned, Hillard and Libby took their vacation in Summer and Harriet and I took ours during the Christmas and New Year holidays.

PHOTOS:

Hillard and me in front of Uncle Harry and Dad's Buick, circa 1928

Al Davidson and me at Ocean Park Beach, circa 1930.

Libby, Hilly, Harriet and me at a Furniture Show in High Point, N.C.

Mrs. Henry Ullman and me in her office at the San Francisco Merchandise Mart.

Big Moves

Nineteen thirty-seven rolled around, bringing big changes in my life. I entered high school and we moved to a different neighborhood.

Mom and Dad had been looking into building a new home, but estimates came back too high every time they put the plans out to bid. Then, all of a sudden, a beautiful house on Lakeside Drive became available at a price dad could afford.

It was a coincidence that the house had been built by the contractor they had favored for the house they had wanted to build. The Lakeside house was unique, with exposed redwood beams embedded in the stucco. It had two nice-size bedrooms upstairs, along with one which was a dormer. The latter was assigned to Hillard and me.

The only inconvenience was that Doralee's room connected to ours by a closet you had to pass through in order to to enter or leave our room.

The room Hillard and I shared was paneled with knotty pine and had a gabled ceiling. It reminded us of a ship's cabin, with its small nautical light fixture hanging from the center beam. I'll always remember the Sunday morning in that room when we heard from our father that Pearl Harbor had been attacked. What a shock!

We always seemed to have company on Walnut Street, but when we moved to the Lakeside house, dad built a huge barbeque pit behind the garage. Soon, he and mother would invite large groups over for Sunday barbecue's. It was great fun for the oldsters as well as the youngsters.

Uncle Mike and Aunt Evelyn lived across the street from us on Lakeside. She became my "listening post" when I needed to blow off steam about my parents, as all teenage kids do. I would join her at her kitchen table and we would drink Nescafe while she smoked and listened. She never offered advice, as she was not a big talker, but just the same, she could often get me to see the other side.

Among my many friends were several of my cousins, but at the beginning of my senior year at Stockton High School, while standing with a group of other students, I noticed a newly arrived student standing all alone and went over to greet him. He turned out to be Marvin (Buddy) Marks, and from that moment on we became the closest of friends. A few years later we enlisted in the Army on the same day and our serial numbers end in 348 and 349 (mine). When we first met, Buddy's father was gravely ill; he and Bud's mother had moved to Stockton to be close to their daughter and Buddy's sister, Lane Fields. Bud's father died shortly afterward, and my dad became a surrogate to him.

We belonged to a Jewish fraternity called Aleph Zadik Aleph (AZA). One of its main attributes was that it created opportunities for Jewish kids to meet one another, particularly boys and girls. As members of this fraternity from ages 14 to 21, we met to discuss ways to help others and have fun. To that end we held regional and national conventions, as well as local dances and outings.

Our regional meetings included Sacramento, San Francisco and Oakland. The national convention was held yearly in a major city such as New York, Washington, D.C. or San Francisco. These conventions began with a Shabbat service on Friday night, but from then on the focus was on debating, sports – basketball and track being the highlights – and, on Saturday night, the big dance. We all dressed up like miniature adults, coats and ties being the choice for boys and long dresses for the girls.

One of the many benefits of belonging to AZA was that many of those early friendships have lasted a lifetime. Some even developed into marriages. I had a crush on the cutest girl. Her

mother liked me, and my grandmother loved her. I even sent her a pair of boudoir lamps from the store. (When we were no longer an item, I wondered what had become of them).

We also learned a great deal about getting along with others who did not share our religious experience. We had interfaith sports at the YMCA, where we played basketball in a league composed of members of various faiths and races. We got along well, and many of those I played against in those days have remained friends to this day.

Among the important things we learned in AZA was the art of disagreeing with one another without resorting to violence. This we learned while practicing debate. Bud Marks was one of the best debaters which foretold that he would become a well recognized defense attorney, whose obituary cited him as being "a tireless defender".

One warm remembrance of those YMCA days had nothing to do with the actual games. I would leave the Y after the game we played against the Chinese Christian Association or some other team and walk the couple of blocks from Channel and San Joaquin streets to Weber Avenue, where my great Uncle, Moishe Sherman, a tailor, had his shop.

Uncle Moishe was the husband of Bashe Corren Sherman, Grandpa Mendel's younger sister and the grandfather of my cousins: Leland

and Ethel Metzger, Leonard and Dickie Burns and others with whom I had little contact.

His shop was on the way to the family store, where I was expected to work on Saturday afternoons, after the Y. It was a very small store front containing a table, a chair, a sewing machine and an ironing board. In my mind's eye, I can still see him licking his fingers and testing the heavy iron.

When I arrived, he would greet me with "Hello, *boychic*," and we would talk things over. I can't remember specifically what we discussed, but the subjects were always interesting to me. When I left, he'd hand me a nickel, almost surreptitious instructing me to buy a cornucopia (an ice cream cone). I believe, in retrospect, that he was so secretive because, in those days a nickel was a real piece of money, and he hoped my aunt wouldn't find out.

Now, every time I stand at an ironing board, I think of this small, gentle, hard working man, who came to this country with nothing, led a simple life and never complained. His accent was pleasing, and each word uttered softly.

PHOTOS:

Our family home on Lakeside Drive
Dad at his barbeque
Cropped postcard photo of the old YMCA building, circa: 1907 . (Courtesy of Alice van Ommeren from her book: STOCKTON IN VINTAGE POSTCARDS
Buddy Marks

School Boy-Soldier Boy

It was the spring of 1942, and the world was full of uncertainty. War was raging in Britain and the fields of Europe, but was just becoming a reality in the United States in the wake of the bombing of Pearl Harbor on December 7th 1941.

Except for the realization that sometime in the future we could be called upon to play our part, Buddy and I continued to be schoolboys with a perfect setup: Since they both worked, his sister and brother-in-law allowed us to use their Ford convertible when we weren't in class, as well as their bungalow. We cruised around town, used the bungalow as a hangout, worked at Leeds Shoe Store, played the pinball machines at Ziegler's Pool Hall, and spent hours at Sandy's Drive-in, a local haunt that featured hamburgers and French fries (along with a greasy odor that could really smell up a kid's clothes). This establishment was owned and operated by Joel "Sandy" Senderov, who would later enter the family by marrying my cousin Janie.

Bud and I were on the Rally Committee, which allowed us to participate to some degree in the school's athletic events. Once, after a humiliating football defeat at the hands of our arch rivals, San Jose State, Bud and I skipped the after-game event, and set out to hitchhike to San Francisco for the weekend. It was late at night

(you could do that in those days) and we weren't having much luck thumbing a ride, but finally a bus loaded with Santa Clara students returning from a victorious game picked us up and took us to their campus. We bunked in the beds of a couple of students who hadn't returned, and became bunk shills for the missing. Later that night we were bed-checked, but fortunately for us and the missing students, only the fact that the bed was filled interested the "Brother" who did the checking. The next morning we had to attend Mass before having breakfast.

I joined a fraternity, Omega Phi Alpha, while at college, and enjoyed the good fun and camaraderie it afforded me while at school.

Many of us, albeit in smaller numbers, still get together once a year in the little mining town of Murphy's, and in recent years I had the opportunity to compete with the late Eddie LeBaron, one of the top professional quarterbacks of all times – pitching horse shoes, that is.

Bud and I also attended classes, sang songs, chased – but didn't catch – girls, cut wax records on the then-popular home recording machine known as the Recordio (the precursor of the various home recording devices which followed), and just plain goofed off.

Our favorite pastime was sitting on the couch in Bud's relatives' living room, listening to the big bands on their phonograph. Our favorites were Benny Goodman, Harry James, Artie Shaw, Tommy and Jimmy Dorsey and Count Basie. While listening to the music, we would stare glassy-eyed at a huge colored photo of the dazzling, red-haired Florence Feingold, the younger sister of my friend's brother-in-law, who was then living in Chicago. We just sat there mesmerized and reminded one another that the first one of us to meet her, would marry her. More later.

Like many other students, we worked in defense jobs during World War II. I worked alongside my dad and uncles, alternating between the Port of Stockton, where we loaded and unloaded cargo, and the Flotil Cannery, where we assumed many roles, volunteering after working hours for the war effort.

During the summer, when school was out, I worked at the shipyards, first at Colbergs and later, when they began building Pollacks – a larger yard – I got a job as a Pile Driver Carpenter's Helper. This required me to supply the men who were lining up the piles and nailing the guides in place. We brought their equipment and drinking water, using very high catwalks to get to them. When my mother got wind of what I was doing, I found myself back selling ladies' shoes at Leeds.

I also worked in the fields baling hay and digging asparagus roots. The hay baling wasn't so bad, although we didn't have the kind of equipment that was available even in those days. Instead we worked with pitch forks, forking the hay into a bailer, then tying the baling wire to create bales. It was grueling work in the hot sun with no shade. We were happy when lunch time came along so we could eat the sandwiches our mothers had prepared for us, and we were even happier at quitting time, when the foreman told us to get on the truck to go back to town. In those days, you just found a spot on the bed of the truck and held on. We had never heard of seat belts, although to my knowledge no one ever fell off.

We were dirty and sweaty, and when we got home a hot shower was a real luxury. I'm reasonably sure that the migrant workers, who sweated alongside us didn't partake of the same luxury.

If I thought baling hay was dirty work, my next job – digging out old asparagus roots on a ranch in the Delta – proved to be even dirtier. The peat dirt was so fine that it got into and under your clothes, which caused unimaginable itching. The shower became a river of black for the first minute or so.

Speaking of the peat dirt, it caused no end of problems for the city because it was so fine it came in through the windows, which weren't as weather-stripped as they are now, and created a layer of black, sooty dust on everything that wasn't covered. Housewives and those who wore white clothing complained about it, as did the Chamber of Commerce and the real estate people. The peat dirt became a stigma for the City of Stockton, and there was great deal of talk about what to do about it, including controlling the planting, tilling and cutting of the crops. Farmers were affected, too, as much top soil was lost to the wind each year, just as in Egypt on the Nile. Finally a solution was found, though it took some time to take effect: Tree barriers against the prevailing wind were planted and the production of white asparagus was discontinued. This solved the problem. (Note: In order for asparagus to be white instead of green, it must be kept out of the sun with mounds of loose peat dirt and this is what blew into town.)

The city, once known as the Peat Dust Capitol, is now known by a few other unflattering names, including The Foreclosure Capitol. (A television reporter from French television was sent here with a crew to report on this phenomenon and Harriet and I became acquainted with her and have visited her and her family on subsequent trips to Paris.)

Time passed, and the breath of the draft became hotter, leading almost all the boys in school to search for a way to forestall the long arm of Uncle Sam. This quest led Bud and me to a school assembly where the Navy and Marines presented a plan offering deferments to students who wanted to join up and would be, in exchange, allowed to finish college. After listening to the speeches, we decided to join the Marine Reserves, or V-12 as it was called. We thought this was a sound plan, since we figured the war would be over by the time we finished school, and why not have the distinction of enlisting in the most daring branch of service?

The catch was, because we were underaged, our parents would have to sign an approval, which they wouldn't. So now the two brave Marine enlistees, who had already begun bragging, were left without a military affiliation and were still subject to the draft.

The prospect of bidding farewell so soon to college life was not very pleasant, so we were thrilled when the Army came up with a reserve program which promised to let recruits finish

HOME ADDRESS REPORT PIT ERC UNSCD
(Complete both forms. See instructions on reverse side.)

NAME Cowen   Melvin   Herschel   California
     (Last name) (First name) (Middle name)   (State, see note below)

RANK OR RATING Private   Stockton
                                                              (City or town, and county)

SERVICE PIT ERC UNASSIGNED   2255 Lakeside Drive
        (Army, Navy, Marine Corps, etc.)   (Street No. or R. F. D. No.)

No. 19,190,349 RACE White   NOTE.—Give home address at time
(Army serial or Navy Service)   of entrance into service.

(This form is not to be used for men inducted into   Melvin H. Cowen
    service through Selective Service)   (Signature)

D. S. S. Form 166—HOME ADDRESS REPORT.   16-16432   GPO college before beginning active duty. It lacked the glamour of the Marines and the crisp whites of the Navy, but it was a hedge, and a way to save face with our fellow students, so we signed up. Our folks couldn't refuse this time since eventually we were going to be drafted and enlisting in the army seemed a safer alternative than the Marines.

We joined the Army Enlisted Reserve Corps (ERC) expecting to stay in school, but, shortly thereafter, we received our marching orders.

In the interim, my parents took me to San Francisco and Los Angeles for a vacation treat, as well as to say goodbye to friends and relatives, who treated me like a celebrity.

It was a wonderful trip, but on March 16th, 1943, shortly after having returned home, we Army Reserve Corps members gathered with our families and friends in front of the gym on campus where two buses waited to take us to the induction center at the Presidio of Monterey.

We were 58 future soldiers, kicking and screaming on the inside, but outwardly displaying the bravado of knights in armor, as we prepared to board the two buses that would take us away from all we were familiar with and drop us into the unknown.

A pall hung over the crowd of fellow students, family members and friends gathered to bid us farewell and good luck. Everyone put on a smiling face and tried to act bravely, but as the buses began to move out, the crowd fell silent

IT'S FAREWELL, BUT NOT TO ARMS

until, in a show of bravado, the college band took up the beat and played patriotic melodies such as, "Over There" (of all the tunes they had to choose from, they chose that one).

We were off to begin our great adventure. Aboard the buses, we looked back on the crowd of well-wishers and realized that all the cheering was a cover for the tears which were soon to flow. A newspaper article the following day describing our departure noted, "The little Corren kids, so proud of Mel, each wanted the last word." *

Following a quiet and apprehensive ride, we arrived at the Presidio of Monterey, where, amid much confusion, we stripped, were examined, shot up with preventatives and introduced to the most important phrase in the Army – Hurry up and Wait. That first night in the barracks, we shared and ate all the goodies our parents had sent with us. We talked about old times, discussed our hopes for our assignments, and finally, those of us who could, fell asleep.

The next day was filled with aptitude testing of every kind which, we discovered, had nothing to do with the duty to which we would be assigned. Finally, on departure day, we were awakened by the blast of a bugle and, for the first time, were introduced to what we would come to accept as part of Army life: "Sweating It Out".

Bud and I were disappointed to learn we weren't shipping out together, but we bravely bid each other goodbye. We boarded trains going in different directions. I had been on a train before,

but never a Pullman Sleeper. Now, as a guest of Uncle Sam, I was on one going all the way across the country to a place called Aberdeen Proving Grounds, near Baltimore, Maryland.

Bud went to Fort Leonard Wood and later on to college under the auspices of Uncle Sam. From college he was transferred to the Medics and shipped to England. Then, after the war, we remained good friends, though never as close as in the days of our youth.

Although apprehensive on the train to Aberdeen, I was also quite excited. I believed – quite prophetically – that this was the beginning of a great adventure in which anything could happen.

I wasn't disappointed, because on the second day out we all lined up at the bathroom door with the first case of the GIs any of us had ever experienced. A few days later, after a million clickety-clacks and an interminable number of card and dice games, I and a few others arrived in Baltimore.

We had several hours between trains, so we went to the YMCA, where we all enjoyed what later became known to us as the four S's: sh-t, shave, shower and shampoo. I remember to this day the feeling of that warm water after those days on the train, and I'm often reminded of that sensation when hearing or reading about victims of deprivation, such as prisoners of war or holocaust victims.

* On June 21, 2003, a group of us E.R.C. veterans organized a 60 year reunion 1943-2003 at the University of the Pacific. It was a very nostalgic affair although only 13 out of 58 original members attended. We had another in 2008 and only 3 of us showed up. What the war hadn't done, the passing years had.

The Basic Training Area of Aberdeen Proving Grounds – where I think they sent me to prove that almost anyone can become a soldier – was a dismal place, made up of long, olive drab, tarpaper-roofed two-story buildings without trees. Not a very welcoming place, although that first night I slept so soundly that the morning found me late for reveille and struggling to pull my pants on as I ran to join the ragtag bunch of civi-soldiers already standing at quasi-attention on the parade grounds.

My first impression of the top sergeant was that he seemed quite friendly as he immediately engaged me by asking if I liked water. When I answered yes, he informed me, with an abrupt change of voice and demeanor, that I was on latrine duty for the rest of the week. That was my introduction to my first sergeant and things went downhill from there. That's not to say he wasn't on my side – he constantly reminded me that he was my best friend and was trying to teach me how to stay alive against all odds.

My fondest recollections of Basic Training were chow, calisthenics, drills and parades. However, I excelled only in chow. I remember going to lunch that first Sunday in camp with a soldier friend from Kentucky and afterward saying how surprised I was that the lamb chops were so delicious. "Dais not lamb chops; dems pohke chops," he informed me. From then on I ate everything.

The places I remember best were the mess hall, where you could eat all you wanted (it was before Hometown Buffet) and the day room, where letters were written, books read, games played, and rumors spread.

The rifle range was not my best shot, as somehow the phrase "kill or be killed" never caught on with me. I did, however, discover that target practice was somewhat sexy, since every time I fired a shot, the sergeant hollered out, "Maggie's Drawers" – a reference to a large white flag that looked like bloomers and was waved wildly by an observer when the target was completely missed.

Off-time was best, because then I could go to Baltimore, a city like none I had ever before seen.

The row houses with their front stoops and the old buildings of red brick intrigued me. I walked around, taking in every new sight, sound and experience and relishing it all. I attended parties at the USO and services at the temple which led to more parties. I was fascinated by the Pennsylvania Railroad trains, which whizzed by so fast we were warned not to stand too close as the speed of the trains creates a vacuum which might pull you right onto the tracks.

The racial segregation in the South was unfamiliar to me, as I had never been exposed to "separate but equal facilities". One day, on a city bus I offered my seat to an elderly black woman. She would not accept and I was read out by the driver who called me a troublemaker and suggested I either sit back down or get off the bus. I told him about all Americans being equal and got off the bus. I can't say that my action meant anything to anyone but me, particularly since the woman continued to stand. However, as I strutted away, I felt about 10 feet tall.

Some time later, I got the shock of my life, when I received this postcard:

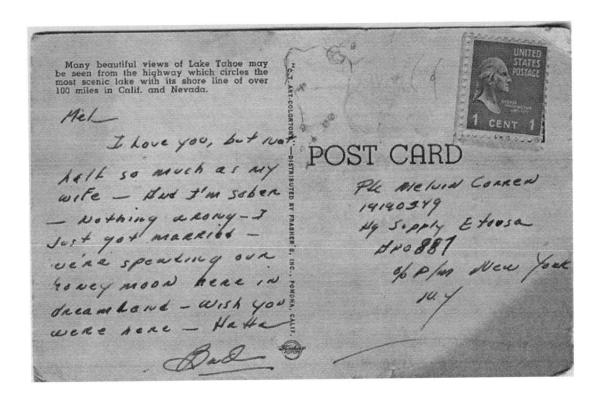

Many beautiful views of Lake Tahoe may be seen from the highway which circles the most scenic lake with its shore line of over 100 miles in Calif. and Nevada.

Mel—

I love you, but not half so much as my wife — But I'm sober — nothing wrong — I just got married — we're spending our honey moon here in dreamland — Wish you were here — Ha Ha

Bud

POST CARD

Pfc Melvin Corren
19190349
Hq Supply E troosa
Apo 887
c/o P/m New York
N.Y.

UNITED STATES POSTAGE 1 CENT 1

Bud had met and married Florence, the dazzling red head in the picture.

PHOTOS:

E.R.C. Enlistment Card
My entrance badge for wartime work
The dazzling red haired girl, Florence
Going off to war in the E.R.C. (Courtesy of The Stockton Record, circa 1943)
Me at "Parade Rest"
Bud Marks
Guess who?
Aiming.
Postcard from Mr. and Mrs. Marks

Post Basic

After eight weeks of basic training, a sign-up sheet was posted in the barracks for all Enlisted Reserve Corps personnel, so inclined, to join the Army Specialized Training Program (ASTP) which was designed to extend Enlisted Reserve status during college. This was the deal: The Army would assign you to the school of its choice where you would always be available for immediate call-up. I didn't opt for this as I had already been selected for Clerk Specialized Training School on the other side of the base. Having experienced the fickleness of the Army, I figured that taking risks with its future decisions would be foolish. It proved a good choice, because many of those who went into the ASTP program were pulled out not long afterward and sent into the ranks as replacements. Many went into infantry units, and, as in the case of my friend Bud Marks, into the medics. In the clerk training program, I learned to type and graduated out as a clerk typist in supply. This certification proved to be quite advantageous, as will be seen later on.

They say the days fly by when you're having fun, and fun I was having while in this program, but then the rumors began to crop up. We were all going to ship out, and the smart money said we were destined for Shenango, PA, where we would board a ship, probably to Africa. This meant that the fellows who lived on the East Coast could see their families before going overseas, but we from the West Coast could not.

The night I heard about our impending journey, I was sitting in the day room and told the fellow sitting next to me how bad I felt that I couldn't see my folks before going overseas. He asked me my name and serial number and told me he worked in the office where the orders were cut and that he'd see what he could do.

The next day, I was surprised and happy to learn that I had orders to go West to join the 478th Ordinance Evacuation Company at Camp Young, at Indio California, for Desert Maneuvers. These maneuvers were designed and instituted by General George Patton who had originally set up and commanded this huge military exercise, but had since left to lead his Army to victory in Africa.

PHOTO:

The insignia of the U.S. Army Specialized Training Program. (From a wartime high of 150,000 students, ASTP was immediately reduced to approximately 60,000 members. The remainder, having already completed basic training, were sent to the Army Ground Forces.)

On The Desert
(The Mojave, that is)

So, as a soldier in search of other places to conquer I left Aberdeen, MD and returned almost home – to Indio, CA – for desert maneuvers with General Patton's Army. It was there at Camp Young that all the maneuvers' stringent rules came into play. The most memorable one was to "sh-t, shave, shower and shampoo" every day using only one canteen of water – a nearly impossible feat in the desert heat.

I joined the 478th Tank Evacuation Company, a newly created organization which I understood was modeled after German General Rommel's modus operandi, in which disabled tanks were winched up on low bed trailers and pulled by armored tractors to the rear to be repaired and returned to battle. The first cabs of these tank-evacuation behemoths were open with a removable canvas top but later models had a cab which, as I remember, was large enough for a crew of four or five, including a driver, navigator, radio operator and one or two mechanics. I believe the 478th was one of the first companies of this type in the U.S. Army.

I personally went on only one or two of those practice runs, but, it is my recollection that I endured the heat and the water rationing moderately well. On these maneuvers I was introduced to the Lister Bag. It was a canvas bag suspended below a tripod and contained water which was treated with a horrible-tasting chemical.

I also remember the combat training which caused us to travel on our bellies under what they said was live machine gun fire. I can't believe they fired live ammunition, since I wasn't killed.

My family used its gasoline ration to pay me a visit, which caused me extra anxiety on the range, since I had to worry that one, I wouldn't keep my head down, and two, if I didn't, I would miss out on all the delicious home baked goods I just knew they were going to be bringing. Fortunately, I lived.

It soon came time for us to leave behind the desert, the sage brush and the snakes to go off to Camp Cooke, where we would await our orders to ship overseas.

PHOTOS:

A later, but similar, model of the Tank Evacuator.

Google: Desert Training Center/California-Arizona Maneuver Area

---

The Patton Armored Museum at Chiriaco Summit, Ca. honors General George Patton and is a memorial to those WWII G.I.s who trained there.

Get Ready Get Set

From Camp Young I went to Camp Cooke at Lompoc, California, where again my folks came, along with a couple of my cousins, to visit me. We had a great time, and as usual, they came with boxes of even more exotic things to eat. My buddies in camp loved it when my family brought or sent me "care packages," as we shared and shared alike. (All during my army experience I received these packages which were put together by members of the family at weekly sessions and sent to Uncle Mike, Uncle Al, Irv, Hillard, and myself.)

Shortly after my family's visit, I got a one-week furlough. Excitedly I boarded a Greyhound bus for a hot crowded ride back home to Stockton.

Although I had only left my hometown a short time ago, it didn't seem the same. It was a strange feeling. Maybe it was the fact that I had been away – kind of on my own – or maybe it was the gnawing knowledge that when I left again, I wouldn't know if I would ever return. There wasn't much time to think about it because the next afternoon I got a phone call to return to Camp Cooke. My unit had received orders to leave. So, smothered with hugs, kisses and tears, I once again left home and joined my comrades in arms.

A few days later I returned to Camp and we boarded a train to Fort Dix, New Jersey, where we awaited orders to board ship. Waiting days were days of inactivity, except for the marching, just to keep us in shape.

Some of us got passes to New York City and stayed at the New Yorker Hotel for $6.00 a night, took in the Stage Door Canteen and enjoyed the USO entertainers, big names all. We also bought and sent home presents from Macy and Gimbels'. We fellows from small-town America were blown away by the size of those department stores and even more so by Grand Central Station and the Empire State Building. Our necks craned ever upwards. While awaiting our orders to board ship, the Army didn't miss a trick. We marched in formation while waiting.

All aboard!

The day to board ship finally arrived. The troop ship, USS Argentina, we were told, had originally been the President Harding of the America President Lines. It was sold off and had been plying the seas off South America before being brought into service as a troop ship. Bombarded with rumors and quasi facts of all kinds, we came to the conclusion that we were headed for Africa.

However, it turned out the African campaign was winding down so our convoy turned mid-ocean and sailed to England, where we were to prepare for the invasion of Europe, known later as D. Day.

We were trained, but were we ready?

As Luck Would Have It

While walking up the gangway of the USS Argentina, one of those small-world happenings occurred. I looked to my left, and there alongside me was a fellow with whom I had gone to Stockton High School. It was Bob, a fellow Tarzan (the High School mascot), whose wife had been a babysitter for my cousin Leonard.

Our meeting was a miracle, perhaps, but it was only the beginning!

At the top of the ramp, I saw a sign instructing all Jewish enlisted personnel to report to the Officers' Mess Hall for a holiday Service. I turned to Bob and asked if he would like to go with me, and he said he would. I didn't think it mattered that he wasn't Jewish, and he didn't have anything else to do, so we enjoyed the service performed by a Lutheran chaplain. (In the service the chaplains of the various denominations often filled in for one another).

I was so happy to be able to attend a service that, with Bob in tow, I fought my way through the other rapidly exiting GIs to the makeshift *bema* (altar). There, I saluted the chaplain, who was a Lutheran minister filling in for a rabbi, and thanked him for doing this service for us. He returned the salute and told us that he appreciated the thanks, and asked if we had been assigned any duties aboard ship. We hadn't, so he gave us each a card with a note to show our commanding officers informing them that we would be the chaplain's assistants for the duration of the voyage.

That card meant that instead of sleeping one night in a stack of four or five bunks and the alternate night out on the deck, as all the other enlisted men had to do, Bob and I were assigned the Red Cross cabin, which was devoted to the library, the PX (where Red Cross cigarettes, candy and games were issued), and – for the lucky chaplain's assistants – sleeping quarters with a private bathroom.

The perks went on: We had a pass which entitled us to eat at any time, bypassing the mealtime line that extended seemingly for miles all around the deck. The soldiers stood in this line for breakfast, lunch and dinner.

Bob and I were assigned the duty of showing first-run movies every night to the officers' in the officers mess. This led to our being able to eat officer's fare after the movie.

This chaplain's note was a tremendous break, and all just for being polite, showing a little appreciation and bucking the traffic.

The card that made it all possible.

On Foreign Soil

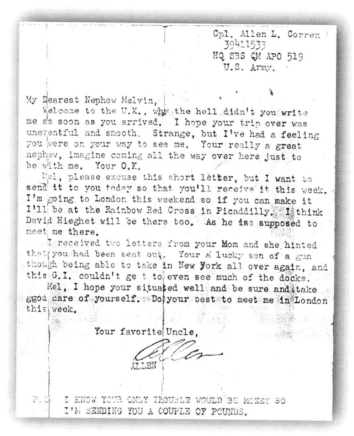

I suppose it's OK to tell you right off that we arrived in England – Liverpool, to be exact – but in those days our destination was a P.O. box and, according to the Army, *that* was where you were. The Army Post Office knew, and, of course, The Phantom. It wasn't until later that Kilroy knew, because "he was there". (Google him)

Another person knew as well, because I received a note from Uncle Alleyboy just after I arrived welcoming me to the UK (I never discovered how he knew). He had thoughtfully enclosed a couple of pounds sterling.

I'll never forget that first train ride from the Liverpool docks to Thatchum, Berkshire, where I would spend the next 10 months getting ready for the planned invasion and liberation of Western Europe. Of course, when I say I'll never forget that train ride, I refer to the fact that as an army travels on its stomach, so was it true of this man's army. There were stops along the way where the Red Cross served us donuts and coffee, and at Salvation Army canteens, where we were introduced to meat pies, offered with tea. I ate them with relish (pun intended) until my soon-acquired English friends told me what they thought might be the ingredients – pigs' ears and snouts. Need I go on?

When we finally arrived at Thatchum, a huge expanse of undeveloped land where a few Quonset huts had been set up, we fell into our bunks for a good night's sleep. In the morning we were told that we would be building a depot for GI vehicles that we would later issue to units arriving from the States. Without further ado, we were handed picks and shovels, put on a truck and driven out to a gravel quarry, where we began loading, seemingly a never-ending series of dump trucks. The trucks, when filled, headed back to the newly designated depot, where another crew spread the gravel, making the area suitable for storing huge number of GI vehicles.

We later found that the kinds of vehicles we stored were service-types, as opposed to combat vehicles, which were stored further south and closer to the Channel in a depot near Tidworth.

Our little depot now acquired a number-name – Sub depot O641 – and our location was at Thatchum, a small village near Newbury, Berkshire, in the south of England. Three towns were within regular pass limits: Thatchum, Newbury and Reading, the latter being the largest of the

three. On longer leaves, we could also go into London and other places of interest. The troops of the 478th Ordinance Evacuation Company were the ones chosen to dig, load the trucks, and spread the gravel at the new depot.

Once the depot was ready to receive vehicles, convoys began arriving from the Liverpool docks, driven by members of our company. I personally went on only one of these convoys, and, except for the Salvation Army stops, it was a bore.

After the vehicles were received (including those of other Allies), they were made ready, which entailed removing the Cosmoline, a heavy, dark grease packed around all the parts that might be affected by the salt water aboard ship.

The types of vehicles we stored were Jeeps and amphibious Jeeps, Dodge ½- and ¾-ton cargo and personnel carriers, personnel and cargo carrying ½-tracks (wheel in front and caterpillar tracks in the rear), 2½-ton General Motors cargo trucks affectionately known as "Jimmies" and shop trucks, which could do all kinds of light to heavy maintenance in the field. The Ducks were amphibious troop carriers and looked very much like their name. We also stored a variety of civilian-type sedans used for officer transportation. Once serviced, vehicles were set in place, ready for the unit to which they were assigned to pick them up. There were occasions when either the vehicles or the troops they were assigned to did not survive the crossing.

We were housed in Quonset huts (large metal drums cut through the center and placed on the ground with the round side up). At the end and middle of each hut there were coal-burning potbelly stoves, which broiled you if you were close, and which you hardly knew were there if you were standing a few feet away.

The latrine and the mess hall were down the road, as were all the work buildings. The odor of burning coal – whatever that chemical formula is – was always in our noses and throats, but we got used to it after a time. As my Uncle Ernest in San Francisco was prone to say, "You can get used to anything, even hanging."

Across from the depot was a huge piece of land filled with huge crates. These were shipping containers for the gliders which had been received for the Glider Troops to use during the planned and promised invasion of Europe. These empty glider boxes were the size of a very large room and were often used as shelter by some of the civilians.

The name of this airfield (base), which would later play a dramatic part in the invasion of Europe– and, much less spectacularly, in my own future – was Greenham Common, which I'm sure had been lovely before all this mobilization, but then it was the site of row after row after row of C-47 troop carriers and gliders, which

had been shipped over from the USA in the aforementioned crates. There were continuos practices of take offs and landings and the drone was sometimes deafening.

Life at O641 was unremarkable except for an occasional air raid alarm when, occasionally, German planes flew overhead on their way to London, just a few minutes away by plane and 40 minutes by train. They never dropped anything on us, but occasionally jettisoned a bomb or two somewhere nearby before going back across the Channel. Toward the end of our stay, we did experience the V-1 rocket. The fear was that the

engine would quit while it was overhead and fail to reach its more strategic destination. This did happen occasionally, but, fortunately, not on us.

We were stationed about 40 miles from London, and relatively safe from air raids, but, whenever we got a weekend pass we headed straight for London where we could expect to be in one. The expression "When in Rome..." applied to being in London. We saw that the English, as difficult as it was to do so, brushed it off and became more determined, so we followed suit.

After the first few raids, when we panicked and sought refuge in bomb shelters, we, too, became hardened and rather nervously laughed it off. For example, on my first pass to London, I was sitting at the bar in the GI Hotel and the air raid sirens went off. I was scared out my wits and didn't know what I should do, so I asked the bar tender where to find the nearest bomb shelter. He looked me straight in the eye and with an upward nod of his head and a sweep of one finger, said, "Tha'll ghao awahy."

We saw many air raid shelters, but the Underground Tube stations, were tragic sights. Those tunnels had become home to many bombed-out victims, who, having lost everything but their lives, were now sharing the only thing left to them, their privacy. There was no sanitation beyond the most basic, and even though these unfortunate victims of vicious and indiscriminate bombings had to rely on others for their day-to-day existence, they didn't lose their pride or resolve. They were Brits – the people who would become known as The Nation That Would Not Bow Down, neither in fact nor spirit!

I came to find this same spirit in the people of Thatchum which was near our depot. Many had come when their homes were bombed out in the East End of London – the section which, until the Nazi bombings, had been heavily populated by London's Jewish population.

Among the Jewish families that had been relocated to Thatchum were Mr. and Mrs. Singer and their two children: Anita, a 15-year-old, and Ivan, her 10-year-old brother, who later proved to be the linchpin in our future relationship.

Next door to the Singers were the Ethertons (she was Mrs. Singer's sister), who had two children, Ivar and Evelyn, who were younger than the Singer children. (After the war they had another daughter, Judy, whom I met many years later on a visit to London.)

In a letter home, I told my parents how I came to know these folks:

Tonight I have a story or two that I'm both proud and happy to tell you, because I know that it will mean a great deal to you to know what happened to me on Chanukah this year (1944). I wrote you the day before yesterday that I received a 24 hour pass starting that evening. I was going to Salisbury to visit Uncle Al, but since public transportation is very limited, it became impossible to go that far, so I was caused, by fate, I suppose, to remain in the small town near our camp. I booked a bed at the Red Cross facility and went to

the cafeteria. As I progressed, in queue, close to the bulletin board, I noted a sign which stated that Chanukah services were going to be held at the Baptist church in the town. I immediately made up my mind to be present for the service and social at 2:30 p.m. the next day.

On entering the church, I noticed two fellows (GIs) who I had met at the Red Cross that morning. We began talking, and I found that they were stationed within walking distance of my camp and they introduced me to the families with whom they came: Mr. and Mrs. Etherton, Mr. and Mrs. Singer, and their children: Anita Singer who was 15 or 16 yrs. old and crazy about America, and her brother, Ivan about 10 yrs. old, and their cousins: 2 other boys, ages 9 and 12, and 2 other girls about 5 and 9. These people are really haimisha mentchen (homey, friendly people).

We enjoyed the services, the kiddies' play and refreshments that followed, and after the affair was over, we all decided to walk "home" together, but on the way, we stopped at one of their homes in the village, Thatchum. where they lived. They invited Charley, Seymour and myself in and they (as would my own mother and grandmother) insisted that we stay for supper.

We went in and were, on the spot, made to feel right at home in their small home (they were relocated from their homes in London during the blitz). We talked about the sinking of the Scharmhorst, and then about America (Anita, or Nita, as she was called, wanted to know everything about the USA, and seemed to be really taken with the idea of someday going there). Then we sat down to fresh eggs and chips (they have a few chickens in the yard), a vegetable salad, pickled herring and a *dessert (fruit tzimmis). Everything was delicious.* *

Their homes on Roman Way in Thatchum were a long but doable walk to our depot, but often we would stay the night in the attic room on a big feather mattress that was so soft and downy it almost enveloped you, in a very welcoming sort of way. I've since attempted to create a similar feeling by using layers of down comforters under a deep-sided mattress pad.

They always had something fresh and good to eat for breakfast which was served to us around dawn. My favorite dish were the big duck eggs with their dark orange yolks. After breakfast we would walk the mile or so back to our base.

There was a market in the center of the village one or two days a week, and these folks had a stall where they sold notions. On occasion, when I had time off, I would help a little in the stall.

A fellow I knew from Sacramento in the AZA (the young mens' auxiliary of the Bnai Brith), went with me to visit with the Singer and Etherton families. He was stationed with a medium maintenance company alongside ours.

When the war was over, both of these families returned to London, and I didn't have an address for them. Fortunately, my parents saved an invitation they had received to the Bar Mitzvah of Anita's brother Ivan on

which the number of the synagogue was printed. Then, when Mom and Dad went to London in 1964 they showed it to the *shamos* (caretaker), who recognized the name and called Mrs. Singer. You can imagine how shocked she was and how improbable it seemed, after all those years, that my parents would be practically at her doorstep. After all, her daughter, Anita, who was about 15years old when we met during the war, had already married Gerry Abrahams and had her own daughter, Gillian and a son, David.

The reunion was later followed by my first revisit along with my wife and mother in 1969. Since then our families have continued a friendship which now spans nearly 72 years and extends to our grand and their great grand children.

PHOTOS:

Letter from Uncle Al
Me and a 478th Jeep
Glider boxes in the field opposite our depot.
Courtesy of : Johnathan Sayers, Thatchum, UK
Anita Singer in 1943
Anita and me Thatchum 1969.(combined photo)
Anita and Gerry Abrahams with their son David (left), daughter Gillian (right) and their spouses, Mitchell and Joy taken at Anita's and Gerry's 50th wedding anniversary in London.

---

* My mother kept every one of my war time letters. I donated the least mundane of them to the Museum of Tolerance in Los Angeles (and as you can imagine coming from an 18-20 year old, many of the others were just that, mundane).

Depot 0641

Getting back to Army life, the following is a broader description of our depot operation. The vehicles we received off the docks in Liverpool had been loaded on cargo ships in the USA with papers designating that they be distributed to specific companies arriving on separate troop ships.

When those troops arrived in the UK and showed us proper identification, they picked up their vehicles and drove them to the place where they were stationed.

We would have received a teletype alerting us as to when they would arrive so we could pull the specifically requisitioned vehicles and have them ready to be picked up. I can't recall any instance at our depot where the vehicles or troops didn't both make the crossing.

The only unpleasant experience I had in Thatchum, or for that matter in my whole Army experience, happened about three weeks after we arrived. One night after a few of the rougher guys returned from a night on the town, one of them came into our hut yelling that he wanted to get the Jew and beat the hell out of him. Being the only one of that particular persuasion in the company, I was scared to death that the whole group would tear me to pieces, but instead the others calmed him down and for the next few days froze him (didn't talk to him). He later apologized to me, saying that he had gotten a little drunk and really didn't mean it. I was relieved that I wasn't ganged up on and happy that the other guys took my side when intolerance could have ruled the day.

Our company consisted mainly of men from the Great Lakes region. They had been selected for this duty because they had worked on the docks around Chicago and Milwaukee and were familiar with the machinery, such as winches and the like, necessary to haul large cargoes.

It wasn't long after that incident that a welcome and fortuitous opportunity arose out of the blue. It was a rather sunny day for England and one that proved even brighter for me when, as usual in the morning, we fell out in formation. After roll call, four names were called out to step forward, mine among them. Once the company was dismissed, we were told we would be attached for temporary duty to the headquarters cadre, consisting of four noncommissioned officers.

We were still assigned to the 478th Ordinance Tank Evacuation Company for administration, quarters and rations, but after that day we had very little to do with the company.

We four, as we were told on the way to our new office, were the only enlisted men in the outfit who had had any college experience, so we were an easy choice.

This turned out to be a turning point for us since, after that morning, we no longer had to stand in formation but went directly to the depot, a very short distance from the barracks, and did whatever was called for during the day.

The four headquarters noncoms in the cadre – who took their orders from the London headquarters – had specific duties. Two administered the office, and the other two were in charge of the vehicle readying and maintenance operation. The light maintenance company, stationed on the other side of the depot did the maintenance work. We four who were attached worked directly under them, keeping the records and issuing vehicles.

The four original headquarters soldiers lived in their own small Quonset hut just behind the depot office and were completely responsible for themselves, except for the fact that they drew their rations (which they cooked for themselves on a small camp stove in the hut) from the commissary at the larger quartermaster depot down the road. They were paid directly from London, and an officer from that headquarters came by about once a month. This officer, who made the rounds of all the sub-depots similar to ours, inspected the operation, issued pay checks and signed blank passes, which could be used by the cadre folks as they chose during the month. We, the "chosen few," soon worked our way into that same independent style of life, even eventually to living in the smaller Quonset hut off the base. It wasn't long before we figured out what a gravy train these guys had, and began

"bucking" for a permanent assignment. Although I believe I was the only one who became a permanent member.

PHOTOS:

Me with Jeep

My shoulder patch designating my membership in the European Theatre of Operations (ETO) Services of Supply (SOS) Seine Section Headquarters.

<u>Note</u>: *I recently emailed a request to use the Glider boxes photo and discovered that the owner, Jonathan Sayers ,is a resident of Thatchum. We've exchanged Emails and he approved the use of the photo*

MEL CORREN

Family Ties In England

Even in England, I had family nearby. My Uncle Allen (Alleyboy) was stationed nearby in Salisbury. We met on pass in London a few times and a couple of times at either of our camps when only one of us had a pass. Once we went to the dog races in Reading, and another time to the horse races in Newbury. On occasion, if we heard that another friend from home was nearby, we arranged to meet him in London, as we did with David Highiet and our cousin Myron Levine, who, as an Air Force pilot, flew gasoline to Patton's army at the front. Dangerous duty, what?

One pass that stands out in my memory was a weekend in London, when Al and I stayed at Rainbow Corners, the Red Cross Hotel, and went out to visit Al's friends the Candys, who owned a kosher restaurant in London. They invited us to their home where we stayed a little too long – Al had to catch the next train back to Salisbury so he wouldn't be late. However, we had to get our belongings at the hotel, so, since I had a longer pass than he, we decided to take a taxi to Victoria Station. The plan was for Al to wait for the train while I went back to the hotel to get our belongings. I did just that, and asked the cabbie to wait, but made the mistake of giving him the fare in advance. When I returned, he had gone and I had to flag another cab, no easy task in those days. I finally hailed on and arrived at the station just as the air raid sirens began blaring. I bought a ticket and bounded through the gate just as it was closing, raced down the platform to the train which had just begun to move, grabbed the bar on the open platform of the last car and pulled myself up with a hand from Uncle Al, who was awaiting my arrival.

As we stood on the rear platform we could see the explosions and flames somewhere in the city as we headed down the tracks.

PHOTO:

Uncle Al and me somewhere overseas.

D-Day, June 5th, 1944

Just as life at Thatchum was starting to seem routine, my old company, the 478th Tank Retriever outfit, was called up and moved out. I, fortunately, stayed behind as an assigned regular in the European Theater Headquarters.

In the beginning, there might have been one or two other fellows left with me and my sergeant at 0641, but after the depot was emptied of all vehicles and the 478th and Light Maintenance Companies had moved out, we two received orders to take the records down to the Ordinance Depot at Tidworth where we had orders to turn them over to the main headquarters.

We left very early on the morning of June 5th, 1944 and, after a short drive, the road became so jammed with vehicles of every type that we had to drive the Jeep off road. Finally, after a long and tedious drive, we arrived, did our duty, and started back to our now empty depot, against the longest line of traffic imaginable.

As we returned to our, now empty, depot O641 we heard the loudest and most persistent drone of airplane engines I believe anyone to this day has ever heard. It seemed we could literally feel the weight of all those men and machines above us as they were making their way east. To add to this bone-chilling drama, as it became darker we could make out the little identification lights on the planes which made them look like swarms of fireflies leaving the airfield.

We had a radio in the Jeep and listened to pilots bidding farewell and tallyho to the controllers as they left the field's airspace. It was eerie to hear little snatches of personal information couched in quasi-military terms, transmitted by the pilots who knew not what their own fate, nor that of their passengers, would be in the next few hours.

By then we were aware that this was D-Day, the day we had all hoped for.... and dreaded: The promised Allied invasion of Western Europe at Normandy.

So with heavy heart, we drove over to a little knoll and continued to watch and listen until the early hours of the morning, whereupon we returned to the silence of our now empty O641 depot.

Later that week we received orders to go to Toddington Manor House, near Cheltenham, a rundown but magnificent place, similar to "Downton Abbey" of TV fame.

PHOTO:

The Manor House (photographer unknown)

Nearly Committed

At this new location we issued trucks – mostly weapons carriers, Jeeps and GMC one-and-a-half ton trucks – to the troops who came to pick up replacement vehicles. The drivers, who were brought down on 6x6 trucks, were prisoners from Army stockades. They drove these vehicles in convoys up to an ammunition dump near Hungerford, where Howitzer shells were loaded aboard. They then drove the load of Howitzer shells down to the Channel and onto barges and other ships, which by that time were plying the waters between England and France on a continuous basis. When the shells were delivered, the drivers were then sent up to infantry companies as replacements.

One memorable evening I arrived back at the depot from a pass in town, debating whether to stop in at the office where the night crew or CQs were minding the store and shoot the breeze for a while, or go right to my quarters. Have you ever felt that you should do just the opposite of what you felt compelled to do? I did on that night, but went all the same to the office, and after just a few minutes, a truck pulled up carrying a frenzied officer and several soldiers. He announced that he was one driver short and needed one of our guys to drive the weapons carrier up the hill to the ammunition dump. He explained that if they located the AWOL guy before the convoy had to leave, he would replace our fellow, but if not, he was commandeering the driver on an emergency basis to drive the ammunition down to the channel and over to Normandy. Who do you think was the only eligible person there not on duty? You're right, 'Twas me."

I sent word immediately to my sergeant that I was being hijacked, but he was not to be found, and the next thing I knew, I was driving one of these pieces of equipment which I had before always received and issued, but not driven.

It was a longer drive than usual, what with all the thoughts racing through my head – mostly fear and recrimination for having stopped at the office against my better judgment.

Morning light brought a wake-up nudge, which was hardly needed, as I really thought that this might be the final chapter of this memoir. I lay awake all night contemplating my fate, and at breakfast, although I didn't have a great appetite, ate like the proverbial condemned man.

Then, just as I finished the last bite, into the mess hall bounced my sergeant in his usual, "cool" manner, announcing that the soldier I was replacing was located and he had brought him up to take my place.

A close call!

D-Day plus Sixty – Over to Valognes

Shortly after the Hungerford incident, things got back to normal, and I had some good times exploring the area. One pleasant day I visited the Cheltenham Fair. I had gone on my own and was enjoying myself, looking at all the wares, when out of the blue, a village lass struck up a conversation with me that probably began with, "Hello, Yank!"

As it is with youngsters on a summer's day, we began to feel comfortable with one another, but since it was growing late, I decided I had better return to the base. So we made a date for the following weekend. She invited me to her home, where she said her folks would, she was sure, be pleased to meet me. We parted in anticipation of meeting again the following weekend, but as fate would have it, a messenger arrived at camp the next day and handed me a TWX. A TWX was – and may still be, for all I know – a military telegram, with orders. These messages often ordered transfers and such, but were usually meant for a group or even a whole company, but when I opened it I saw, where there would normally be a list of many names, only mine.

This order commanded me to move on. So, lamenting the lost weekend, and wondering what that lovely Gloucestershire lass would think of the Yank who didn't show up, I bid farewell to my garrison equipment and proceeded the next morning by Jeep and driver to a designated rail head. There we waited for a train which would take us to an undisclosed destination.

It finally arrived, and took us to a place I recognized as Greenham Common Air Base, the same field from which all those planes and gliders of the 101st and 428th Airborne had taken off just 60 days before.

At Greenham, we detrained and walked – I don't think in any sort of formation – until we arrived on the tarmac of the airport. There we assembled into a huge formation that broke up into smaller alphabetic sub-units. We then lined up to exchange our British pounds into a currency called Invasion Money and received a little booklet telling us how to behave in France.

After this procedure the head honcho, a general, and many lesser ranked officers began reading out the information on the General Order and calling off the names, each soldier shouting "Ho!" when his name was called. After what seemed like hours, all the names had been read off – except mine. When the officer asked if anyone had been left off, I raised my hand and was ordered up to the front and shown to the officer in charge. When I showed him my TWX, of which he had no copy, he couldn't believe it. I was surprised when he asked me if I wanted to go along with them. It was, of course, a rhetorical question. I answered, "Yes, sir," mostly because I had no real choice, but also because I had already exchanged my money and given away all my fancy garrison equipment.

I had never before flown in an airplane and, although it wasn't exactly first class, it was far better than a landing craft. We sat just like the paratroopers, in rows on each side of a C-47 (the predecessor of the civilian DC 8). It was exciting and overwhelming to see the English Channel completely covered with ships and boats of every type, and, on the French coast, a huge floating dock. From the air, it seemed as if a person could walk from boat to boat across the Channel as easily as crossing a very wide bridge.

We landed at a little air strip and were immediately trucked to a bivouac – a field covered with tents. This would be our home for several weeks, during which time we formed a headquarters that would ultimately be the Communication Zone Services of Supply Headquarters of the European Theatre of Operations in the Seine Section. The brochure which was later printed indicated there were 32 officers and 105 enlisted men in the second detachment who flew to Cherbourg to begin this headquarters cadre. When I consider that I was one of the only 105 G.I.s selected for this incredible experience, I often wonder incredulously, against what odds?

Most of the time we spent in the Normandy countryside was devoted to marching around the infamous hedgerows which served as natural defenses for the Germans and created so much havoc for the GIs in the battle of Normandy. This marching was meant to keep us active while we were not doing whatever we were supposed to be doing to become the future headquarters for supply in Paris.

To ease the monotony there was a farmhouse with barrels of apple cider in the yard. The cider was great if you didn't mind standing in a long line, all the while fighting off the bees and flies. The scuttlebutt was that next door there was a thriving business designed to alleviate the loneliness of the G.I.s so far from home. I personally couldn't understand how they could have had any customers, since the other GIs must also have seen the same basic training movies concerning V.D. as I did.

The most memorable thing that happened to me in Valognes was when we were joined by some new troops. Among them was a fellow from New York by the name of Bob Rieders. He and I would become best friends in the Army, and until his death in January 2016, we stayed in touch by telephone and visits from time to time.

We did some office work, which I cannot even recall, but it had to do with our eventual move to Paris when it became liberated. We were excited, to say the least, about going into Paris, and felt the great day of liberation couldn't come soon enough.

PHOTOS:

Exterior and interior of a C-47 transport plane (Wikipedia: These images or file is a work of a U.S. Air Force Airman or employee, taken or made as part of that person's official duties. As a work of the U.S. federal government, the image or file is in the public domain.)

PARIS - "City of Light"

We waited impatiently until August 25th 1944, when General de Gaulle and his army marched down the Champs Elysees, marking the liberation of Paris. Twelve days afterward, I was in a GMC truck on my way to Paris to join the Seine Section Headquarters Services of Supply for the European Theater of Operations. We were about to enter this grandest of cities to begin a wonderful experience, which none of us in our wildest dreams could ever have imagined.

We rode along the French countryside, facing each other in rows along both sides of the truck. We had been instructed by the officer in charge to leave the

back curtain down. We were like horses with blinders on, moving along, knowing we were going somewhere, but not able to see where.

We finally entered the great city and it was love at first sight.

Our first view was of the Palais de Chaillot in the Place de Trocadero across the Seine from the Eiffel Tower. The driver pulled right up on the lawn, and the officer again told us to stay put and not lift the curtain. He and the driver then went off to find out where we were to report.

They had been gone no more than 10 minutes when there was a knock on the tailgate, and, despite the officer's admonition to the contrary, the guy closest to the back lifted the curtain. There stood a little fragile man on a bicycle, who asked, "*Schprect Deutsche?*" No one answered. "*Parlez Francais?*" Same response. Then he asked, "*A mitzen reihdt Yiddish? (Someone speaks Yiddish?)*" I was the only Jew in the group and answered, "*Ich reihdt Yiddish* (I speak Yiddish)." "*Kum aroyce* (Come out)," he said.

I replied, "*Ich ken nit, mine officier haught mien gezuct as mi daft shtain doh.* (I can't – my officer told us to stay here)," to which he answered, "*Vos mainst du? Kum aroyce!* (What do you mean? Come out!)" By this time it was an open truck. All the guys wanted to know what was going on and, except for me, were out on the lawn.

I couldn't believe that this man, who was one of the lucky ones to have survived and who had been virtually hiding out for four years, could already have a sizable souvenir shop on the rack behind his bicycle. It offered French pictures, Eiffel Tower fountain pen holders, postcards, you name it. He had acquired his inventory in less than 12 days of freedom. He sold his entire stock of merchandise to my comrades within a few minutes, as these guys who had had nothing recently to spend their money on except apple cider, were hungry for souvenirs.

Soon all of my comrades in arms had gone off to explore, leaving only the "shopkeeper" and me standing there.

He then invited me to his house to meet his sister who was in their apartment not far away. I told him again that my officer had told us to stay put, but he had only to point to the empty truck to persuade me to come along.

When we arrived at his place, I found this man, his sister, and their mother – all of them quite emaciated – had been living for four years in the kitchen and breakfast room of an apartment.

With as little as they had, they wanted to share some of their food with me, but of course I refused. After visiting for a while, I told them I had to go back to my officer.

The man began to escort me to the Metro, instructing me to stay on the train until the end of the line (Trocadero). Before we parted he told me he owed me something special because I had interpreted for him so my buddies could buy his wares.

We went to a bar and were having an aperitif when suddenly, through a curtain behind the bar, a man emerged buttoning up his trousers. My newfound friend then poked me in a knowing way and informed me in Yiddish that it was my turn and his treat.

In English, I told him, "No, thank you. I've seen those GI (VD) movies," and left him sitting on the stool, wondering what I had said.

PHOTO:

The Eiffel Tower (A photo I took in Paris)

The First Day I Met Paris

After leaving my newfound *lantzman* (fellow Jew), I boarded the Metro. As I rode back to the Trocadero, where I had left the truck and my fellow soldiers, I reflected on the fact that it was just 12 days after the liberation, and – contrary to what it would be in the near future – it seemed I was the only GI on the Metro train. I felt as if I were the main character in a dream – a stranger in a wonderful place, experiencing something very special.

I couldn't sit still. I felt compelled to walk around to observe what was going on around me. When I reached the back of the train, I came upon a man dressed just like you'd envision a diplomat in an overcoat with a velvet collar and set out as trim and neat as a pin. He was seated at the rear of the last car, a dictionary in hand, which he used to engage me in conversation. This brought to my mind the little booklet which we had received at the airfield before flying to France. An entire chapter was devoted to warning us that there would be collaborators seeking GI uniforms to use for smuggling German soldiers out of the city. It warned us that, if we fell into their hands, we could end up with a knife in the back and our bodies floating naked in the Seine. As I looked at this impeccably dressed man, who introduced himself as Georges, I just had the feeling that he was one of those people. Nevertheless, we conversed through the dictionary for several minutes until the loudspeaker announced that the Metro was closing for the night. This, the Trocadero station, was the end of the line.

On exiting, I began to feel a bit more secure since I recognized the place where I had last seen our now long departed truck and told the man with whom I had been conversing that I was going out to look for some night life, and maybe find a girl. It was a lie, but I told him that to get out of a situation I had decided was too dangerous.

He informed me that there was still German resistance across the river, on the Left Bank, and that I would be safer with him. So there I was, not knowing the Left Bank from the Right, but suspecting that this was a story he had concocted to get me to stay with him for the sake of my uniform (over my dead body, I believe, is a correct statement here).

The sound of small arms fire, coming from across the river, convinced me that perhaps the best choice might be to take my chances with him.

As we walked away from the Metro Station, the two of us must have looked quite comical, for, in true Laurel and Hardy, Peter Sellers and Woody Allen fashion, we walked and dodged from tree to tree until we reached greater shelter at the sides of the buildings across the way.

We then reached a set of elegant wrought-iron doors through which he led me, past an elaborate cage elevator (awaiting the war's end and the return of electric power) and up an equally elaborate wrought iron staircase. It seemed like a long climb to the second floor as I thought of all the possibilities that might be in the offing. To add to the suspense, we stopped at a door, where he tattooed a signal-type knock. This display of cloak and dagger made me even more apprehensive about my immediate future. I didn't have long to contemplate because from the other side of the door came an equally unsettling coded response. My newfound friend then announced that he had returned with an American soldier.

At this point my stomach flipped back to where it had been when it had overturned earlier, however once inside, I saw there was a woman, introduced as his wife, and a young boy of about 15, who was introduced as his stepson. They greeted me as the hero I wasn't, but since no one was the wiser, I was only too happy to accept the accolades. The very fact that they appeared to be a family and seemed genuinely happy to see me caused my suspicions to subside, albeit not entirely.

There followed the usual salutations and questions, answered with a dictionary, and afterward a meal that employed a K-ration as its base and leeks as the main ingredient.

This sparse but nevertheless delicious repast was enjoyed in a spacious dining room, at a lovely table and I must add that the K-ration was grossly outclassed by the greens and the talent.

We talked for some time, and after a while I was shown to the study. It was a handsome room, furnished with a walnut desk, a comfortable leather chair and a couch which would serve as my bed for the night. I must admit that I was still quite skeptical, although somewhat assuaged. Although to say I spent a peaceful night would be to ignore the fact that I slept with one eye open.

When morning finally arrived, their son guided me to a garage on Rue Fresnel (a street which ran into the Trocadero), where he had seen American soldiers congregating the day before. Sure enough, that was where I was supposed to be.

After that night we became good friends and I learned that Georges had, before the war, been an electrical engineer and later an officer in the French Army. He had been captured and spent some time in a German POW camp where he contracted Tuberculoses. After the war Georges became a member of the French Army of occupation and was stationed in Germany. My last belated correspondence was returned unopened and marked *décédé* (deceased). I've inquired about them, at their former address during future visits to Paris, but have learned nothing.

PHOTO:

Trocadero Metro station (photo I took recently).

An American in Paris: Me

As one of the first AWOLs to show up at our designated base, you can imagine the welcome I received from the officer in charge. There was talk of courts-martial and the like, but I/we were mercifully spared this harsh punishment. Instead, we spent the next week carrying five-gallon Jerry cans (gasoline cans) up from the basement. Very light punishment indeed for not obeying our officer and for staying away the night before.

When that week was finally behind us, we set to work in earnest. The building on Rue Fresnel in which we were to work for the next year and a half had been a garage and vehicle repair facility for the German army, hence the gasoline cans. However, we would use it as a storage warehouse for class 2 and 4 supplies. This classification denoted expendable items such as enlisted men's and women's underwear, socks, silk stockings, sweaters, jackets, pants, shirts, paper products such as toilet paper and office supplies. In other locations within the scope of our organization were stored small arms, gasoline and heating materials such as coal, and oil.

Some of us did grunt work, others were drivers, and a few got office assignments. The office duties included receiving and issuing supplies, communicating between the branches, and inventory control and operations. At first, I was assigned to a general clerking job, which meant that I was used wherever needed. After a couple of months, I was assigned, with a small group, to a very posh office which was set up under a colonel whose name I can't recall. It was in a very attractive building on the fashionable Avenue Kleber.

I worked directly under a first lieutenant with whom I had worked before. Besides the two us there was one other GI, one or two WACs, and three French girls who could speak English to some extent (among them Janine Roubert, about whom you will hear much more in later chapters).

This office was devoted to the inventory and control of all the expendable supplies used by the U.S. Armed Forces in the Paris area. Our job was to send out inventory teams, receive reports, compile the result and turn the information over to the head quartermaster office, which would then order what was needed to keep the machine running.

Our small group was billed in residence at 57 avenue d'iena,

about a block and a half from the Arc de Triomphe. (On future visits to Paris I visited the location and discovered it to be a Rothschild bank and later the offices of a large Legal firm.)

Every morning we would awake, shower in a public shower a block or so away, then go over to the Champs Elysees where we would breakfast in one of the famous sidewalk cafes, and afterward walk to the Rue Fresnel, passing the Palais De Tokyo, a museum of modern art that in itself was a very modern building. We then descend a very long stairway to arrive at the Rue Fresnel, which paralleled the Seine. It was just like having a regular civilian job, but without having to decide what to wear each day. What a life. As is said in the army, "We found a home."

For a few days we were billeted in a school dormitory, after which we were ensconced in a town house which was probably a beautifully adorned residence prior to the occupation and was just a short walk from the Arc de Triomphe. Though the tapestries, art, rugs and furniture had all been removed, with its fine moldings, marble bathroom and grand staircase it was still a lovely place. We were told that the youngest member of the family who had lived there was rescued by the concierge of the house and hidden away throughout the occupation. I do recall seeing a young boy playing in the courtyard area while we were there.

Now, fast forward approximately fifty or so years when my late cousin Irving Corren and I revisited this building, now a bank. (The two of us had met there many years before and were reliving our pasts). As we stood in the courtyard of what was then my billet and now a bank, a couple of well dressed men approached and asked us what business we had there. I told them my story about being billeted there during World War II and the story we had heard about the young boy. They responded by telling us this young boy was now the chairman of the bank.

Of particular note was a meeting we soldiers had in the bathroom that first night in our billet on Ave d'Iena. We were trying to figure out a use for the strange appliance facing the stool. It was about the same height, so it could have been a urinal, a place to wash your feet or have some other mysterious use. When we got out into the real world and asked questions, we were shocked to discover that Americans didn't know or have everything.

Along with this discovery was another very civilized one which we found to be quite accommodating when in need. It was

the *pissoir*. This famous convenience stop, available in many strategic spots throughout France, has lately been replaced by a newer style which is coin operated and self cleaned after each use by an automatic flushing and cleaning mechanism.

As we became more familiar with the depot at Rue Fresnel and felt increasingly freer to roam the general vicinity, we came to realize just how fortunate we were to be in this renown city and began to feel the aura of the place which we had all read about and seen pictures of, but never thought we would ever experience.

I walked the streets as if I were the main character in a story book, observing everything and trying to understand how I fit into this stroke of good fortune. Most of the time I could almost forget that I was there as a soldier, and often times thought myself the "American in Paris" of movie fame. So, putting myself in character, I would sometimes feel like "soft-shoeing" down

the streets, and at other times I quietly did.

That is, until one day, just at the beginning of my stay, I came upon a display of anti-semitism, in the Palais Berlitz, so offensive that looking at the brochure I picked up that day still makes me cringe. It was titled "*Le Juif et la France*" (Google it) and was removed very soon after.

The next time I heard or read anything about this repulsive exhibition at the Palais Berlitz

was when I read the book: *Sarah's Key* by Tatiana de Rosiny, some 68 years later.

In keeping with the above, when I was stationed at a former Rothschild residence in Paris, I wondered what had happened to the coverings (tapestries), which were missing from the walls. I've recently discovered the. probability while reading *The Monuments Men* by Robert M. Edsel. On page 342, he states that at Buxheim, a Nazi storehouse of looted art, the floor was covered with piles of rugs and tapestries, "many stolen directly from the walls and floors of the various Rothschild estates."

The Nazis stole everything of value from the countries they defeated with the intention to create a super museum of all the greatest art in the world. (That is, except for what the hierarchy had greedily earmarked for their own individual collections.)

When reading this book and realizing the extreme effort and expense that went into the murdering of millions and the relocating of this vast amount of items, it makes you wonder what might have been if they had used all that wealth, energy and manpower toward the defeat of the allies (google Nazi Plunder).

PHOTOS:

Me in front of the fountains in Place Concorde Avenue d'Iena.

Doorway to 57 Ave d'ien

Pissoirs *in Paris, circa 1943 and present (Public urinal photos by author)*

Le Juif et La France at the Palais Berlitz *(Attribution: Bundesarchiv, Bild 146-1975-041-07 / CC-BY-SA 3.0)*

The First Jewish Holidays
After the Liberation

After the liberation, and those dark years under the German occupation were over, the Jewish High Holidays were once again being observed at the famous Rothschild Synagogue on the Rue de La Victoir. There Allied soldiers, along with those Parisian Jews lucky enough to have survived, came together to worship.

Bob and I were among the many who both sadly and joyfully attended that gathering of the remnants of the Jewish people in France. The front pews of the synagogue were left empty in memory of the deportees who would never return. This display of reverence and acknowledgment caused tears to well up in the eyes of many of those in the crowd.

Along with Parisian Jewry were Allied Servicemen of all types and uniforms, including the top brass of the European Allied Command. When the *kaddish* (the Hebrew memorial prayer) was recited on that memorable night, the feelings it evoked were beyond description. I felt they included grief, thanks, disbelief and a good measure of guilt. The latter, we later understood, was suffered by many of those who survived while family members and friends had perished.

The next week was Yom Kippur and our bulletin board was posted with three or four synagogues where we could attend services. We decided not to go to the Rothschild Synagogue again, opting instead for a smaller one. We took a taxi or maybe a Jeep to a location shown on our map but got lost. Finally, a man came along and in broken English/Yiddish asked if we were Jewish and were looking for the synagogue. I told him in Yiddish that we were, and he took us on foot through a few short streets to a *shul* near the Bastille (before the war this was a very Jewish neighborhood in the center of Paris). The services were already in progress, so we took a seat amid welcoming stares from the congregation.

Afterwards, the rabbi asked the congregants to welcome the American soldiers present and invite them to their homes for the *uhp fahst* (the breaking of the fast). Bob and I walked to the rear of the room where we were immediately surrounded by a sea of people asking such questions as: "Do you know *Abe Epstein* from Chicago? My uncle *Eliazer Rosenbladt* who lives in New York; do you know him? I have a cousin in Los Angeles," and on it went. These folks had no idea of the immensity of the United States and, besides, I think they wanted to create an identity and maybe even make contact for future emigration.

Suddenly, an immaculately dressed man pushed his way through the crowd, yanked on Bob's sleeve and said in broken English, "My name is Leon Rosenthal. You come with me. My wife speaks English!"

Bob led him through the crowd to me, and we explained that we were a pair and wanted to stay together. He told us that it was not a problem – we could both come. He explained that his wife, who was from England, would be thrilled to have English speakers in their home. (Can you imagine a young English/Jewish woman coming into that hornet's nest as a bride?)

This was to be the start of another chapter in our Parisian experience.

After stopping for an aperitif, we reached his apartment, where we found his wife, Flossie and their son, Michel (Michael), awaiting the arrival of their husband and father.

When she saw us, we fell into each others' arms and proceeded to talk, eat and drink. That night, they gave each of us the yellow Star of David patch they had been required to wear on their clothing to identify them as *Juives* (Jews) during the Nazi occupation. I sent mine to the Skirball Museum of

the Hebrew Union College in Cincinnati by way of our friend Judy Lucas, the curator.

I explained that the star was given to me by a couple who had survived the four years of occupation in their apartment in Paris. They had taken their baby out for a walk so were not at home when the trucks came by to pick up the Jews in the neighborhood. Fortunately, their neighbors did not turn them in to the Gestapo. They told us how difficult it was with their infant son cooped up in their small apartment, and how, at times, they had to put swaddling cloth in their baby's mouth so as not to call attention to themselves.

Leon's former boss, owner of a tailor shop, risked his life by bringing him work and returning, with food, to pick up the finished products. It was a Schindler-type operation on a small scale. In this case, one hand washed the other, but there would have been serious consequences had they been caught. We met others who told similar stories. (These acts renewed my faith in humankind.)

During our stay in Paris, Bob and I enjoyed many visits with these folks. When we visited Paris with my mother in 1969, we sadly discovered that Flossie had died of breast cancer and Leon was remarried to Noel, a lovely woman who gave us a beautiful music box in the

shape of a piano. Noel's daughter was married to a Spaniard and lived in Spain. This accounted for the fact that on a future trip we visited Leon in Pau, a picturesque city in the Alps, southwest France, near Spain. We heard later from our friend, Janine, in Paris who heard from his son, Michelle, that Leon passed away shortly after we left.

PHOTOS:

Photo of the Rosenthals and us and Scanned Star of David patch I gave to the Skirball Museum at the United Hebrew College in Cincinnati.
Photo of piano music box.

"Livin' Large"

After a few weeks, we began living a remarkably normal life – for soldiers, that is. We awoke around 6:30 or 7:00 in the morning, had no reveille or formation of any kind, got up, dressed and went off to the mess hall, which was a restaurant on the Champs Elysees. We had passes for one or two of the typical ones you see on all the travel posters. There we sat at outside tables in mild weather, had French male waiters, etc. All my visitors, such as cousin Irv and Uncle Al, wanted to pay the check each time we went to eat. When I told them it was GI, they thought I was just trying to be a good host.

In Paris, there was plenty of entertainment for the troops, and all of it first-rate. We had ballet, opera, movies, dancing halls, G.I. cabarets and especially the famous USO traveling shows.

On one occasion, we were awaiting the arrival of Glenn Miller, the famous band leader, who never arrived. We later learned that he had been lost over the English Channel.

One day I found myself in a very lovely antique shop where I bought a pair of metal statuettes purported to have been from a chateau in the Basque region of France. They were fitted for gas light and had been used at the bottom of a staircase on the newel posts. I had them boxed by the prisoners of war from other countries (who had been left behind by the Nazis) and shipped home, along with other souvenirs, to my folks. (The V-mail letters I sent home concerning these statuettes were heavily damaged. I assume they were salvaged from some type of transport that was damaged while carrying the mail. My parents must have thought the worst when they received them, but happily the letters saw more action than I did.)

The first few weeks we sought and found places to get our laundry done, our hair cut, film developed and printed, along with other services necessary for comfortable urban life. Besides walking, the Metro was our main means of transportation. Occasionally, however, Bob and I were able to use the officers' taxicab service. This was the same one that the German officers had used, employing the same Citroen and Renault cabs and buses, as well as the same French chauffeurs. Most of the vehicles had a charcoal-burning apparatus hanging along the side, which created the energy they ran on. This taxi arrangement landed us in the only crossfire fight we ever experienced.

PHOTOS:

The two statuettes I bought in Paris (Author's collection)

Next page: My damaged V-mail letter home

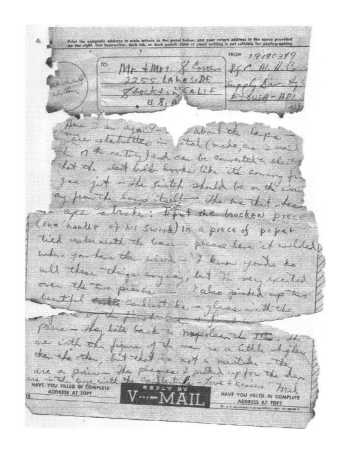

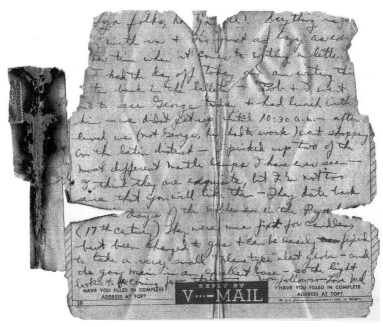

A Scary Encounter

Bob Rieders, with whom I was stationed in Paris, wrote the following account of a scary encounter we shared:

I remember that night vividly. It was just after Yom Kippur, and we were returning to the billet in a taxi when I saw some small-arms fire coming from the rooftops (The FFI and the Free French army were still fighting for the control of Paris). You were on the street side in the back seat next to me, and I was behind the driver. I looked out my side window and saw streaks of light whistle by. It dawned on me that these were tracers, and when I looked up to the driver, he was gone. I said, "Mel, let's get the hell out of here. If one of those tracers hits the gas tank... POW!"

We got out of the car, and I remember crawling along the curb until we reached the door of a house. We got up and made a mad dash for the door, which the occupants opened for us. We got cheers and applause for our daring do!

I remember it. What I can't remember is how we were able to get a cab at our beck and call.

The same night, when things quieted down, we were stopped in the same cab at a road block and taken to the precinct station house because our taxi driver still had a Nazi driver's license.

Here's my memory of the same event:

The FFI (Free French Forces, the renowned resistance group), which was helping to keep order as well as to punish collaborators, suspected us of being Germans in GI uniforms and began shooting at us. I was sitting to the right of Bob, and he was the one in the line of fire, so I was oblivious to what was going on until he yelled something like, "Hey! They're trying to kill us!" We were next stopped at a road block which was very much like a barricade and taken to a gendarme station because our driver had not yet traded his German license for an American one.

They took us into a room and interrogated us in French – which we didn't understand – until somehow they realized we were who we claimed to be. After a short time that seemed like days, we were allowed to continue back to our billet.

It was scary because during those early days of the liberation there were punishments, including head-shaving of female collaborators, as they tried to ferret out and give traitors their due.

Many years later I was informed by a friend (who had heard it from an English woman whose husband helped liberate Belson Concentration Camp), that the head-shaving was why many European women adapted short haircuts right after the war – to show sympathy, or at least empathy, for the female collaborators whose heads were shaved to shame them

One night, instead of a taxi cab, we were picked up in a large, well-lit GI bus. This was very scary because it made us, the only occupants beside the driver, wonderfully illuminated targets. We sat next to the windows, like two birds in a well lit cage within sight of cats. This in itself worried us, but what we were not aware of at the time was even more grave. The mission of this bus was to pick up the walking wounded from a hospital train just arriving at the Gare St. Lazarre, a railroad station in the center of the city. We sat on the bus for a long time while they loaded the wounded. After leaving the station, we headed for the Arc de Triomphe, where Bob and I got off.

These were very similar memories of the event written 60 years later.

PHOTO:

Bob Rieders (Author's photo)

The Roberts

I met Janine Roubert when I went to work in the inventory and control office on Boulevard Kleber. She was a civilian office clerk, and we became friendly when she mentioned she enjoyed opera. I told her how my father sang as a youngster with Professore Flavio Flavious, who was the Italian consul and impresario in my hometown. This colorful gentleman of the old school, with a waxed and pointed mustache and Borcelino hat, attended to the needs of the Italian immigrants, was the agent for the Italian Steamship Co., and publisher of the Italian newspaper *Il Sole*. He was a very good friend of the family's, particularly Grandpa Mendel, who was himself a devotee of the opera.

My father had one share of "Il Sole" stock, which I later donated to the Haggin Museum in Stockton, along with a photo of the Professor's singing group. This troupe of youngsters – who, except for my father, were all Italian – sang arias during World War I to benefit the Italian Red Cross. My father's favorite aria was "La Donna Mobile," the tenor's aria. After I told

this story to Janine, she invited me to go to the opera with her and some of her friends. We had a great time. I remember sitting high up in the balcony that looking down made me dizzy.

Our friendship lasted well beyond her employment in the office, and Janine's mother treated me like a member of the family. I had a standing invitation to their home.

Sundays were particularly wonderful at their apartment. The festivities would begin around 11 a.m. with whoever was invited, usually about four of Janine's friends, including other GIs on occasion, and often an older person. Many were intellectuals and had interesting ideas to discuss. As time went by, I found myself increasingly able to understand the French, since all of my new friends were eagerly helping me learn the language. Generally they spoke better English than I spoke French –

except for Janine's mother and father, who spoke no English and continually challenged me to speak solely in French.

Food was an important part of the Sunday rendezvous, and we began eating soon after we arrived. Coffee and a roll were served first, and a little later in the conversation, a full-blown *dèjeuner* (lunch). This usually consisted of delicacies made in a kitchen the size of a small walk-in closet. Some of the dishes I had not ever heard of, much less tasted.

I remember having a discussion with Janine's father about a food that had the same name in English as in French but was a totally different dish in France than in the USA. Here is how I found out about this difference. He had asked me the week before if I had ever eaten snails, and I had answered that I really liked them, explaining that in America we ate the round, flat, coiled pastries with raisins in the morning with our coffee. He told me he had never heard of that kind, but that he ate the type found in gardens. I made a face and told him I would never eat one of those slimy creatures.

The next week they passed an appetizer of "oysters" baked in butter and garlic. I really liked them. When the plate was empty, Janine's father took me into the minuscule kitchen and showed me a pail full of snail shells. He then made a point of telling me that I had eaten practically all of

them, since they were all in cahoots and had sent the dish to me repeatedly. I was taken aback for a minute, but from then on, I ate a new kind of snail — and tasted many other new and gourmet foods as well.

Janine's family had a small cabin on the Marne River where Janine's father raised snails, which he cultivated for the table. I learned how the snails first go up a slanted, slotted or mesh incline, losing all the slimy stuff in the process, and then are prepared for the table in a mixture of butter, parsley and garlic, stuffed into the empty shells and baked for a time. *Voila!* A delicacy is born, one that, since its exposure to the World War II GIs, has been hailed worldwide as the hors d'oeuvre of choice among folks in the know.

Unfortunately Janine's mother passed away shortly after the war. On her death, her corset shop fell to Janine, who was not a corset maker, so she converted the shop into a boutique she named Mathilde's, after her mother. She worked there seemingly day and night for close to 50 years.

Janine divorced early but continued to live in the same small apartment on the Blvd. Pasteur with her daughter, Laurence.

We renewed our friendship with Janine in 1969 when my mother treated Harriet and me to a trip to visit our son, Howard, who was studying in England. Howard had gone to the shop on a previous visit, as I had instructed, but was told by a very young Laurence that no one answering his description of her mother was still there (her mother was away from the shop and Laurence was skeptical of Howard with his long hair). I, however, felt I had to make sure. So later, during our visit to England, Mother, Harriet and I went over to Paris and sure enough, when I approached the shop window, there was Janine, who almost fainted when she saw me standing there as Laurence had not told her about Howard's earlier visit which she had discouraged. Since that day we have had many visits with Janine and Laurence and her family both in Paris as well as in Stockton.

When Janine closed the shop at the turn of the century, she bought a condominium just behind the Gare Montparnasse in virtually the same neighborhood. Meanwhile, Laurence married Jean Pierre and the relationship expanded to include their children, Celine and Frederic.

Now, Celine is married to Quentin Delot, and, with the recent birth of their daughter, Margaux, a new generation has begun. Sadly, Janine died a few months before Margaux was born, thus depriving her the joy of being a great grandmother.

On a recent visit to Paris, I visited Janine's grave and met Margaux, the great-grand daughter she was destined not to know.

A re-run of the past and a joyful glimpse of the future.

PHOTOS:

Janine Roubert (Photographer unknownA share of "Il Sole" stock

Professor Flavious and his group (Sam Corren 2nd from left, second row) (Photographer unknown)

Janine and her parents at their place on the Marne River. (Photographer unknown)

Janine's mother in front of her Corset Shop

(Photographer unknown)

Harriet and me with Janine's family in front of her shop, Matylde

Harriet, me, Laurence in back and Frederic, Celine and Janine in front.

Celine, Quentin and Margaux. (A selfie)

Family Ties in France

During WWII Uncle Al and I visited together many times in England. Then, when we both arrived in France, we continued our visits. With me stationed in Paris and him in Rheims, it was easy to travel either way. Together we saw many historic and beautiful things, including magnificent cathedrals, palaces, and museums. We also visited with folks who had befriended me. It was like a touch of home having him so close, and every one of our visits was heartwarming.

When cousin Irving arrived in France, he sent me a letter extolling the virtues of Lucky Strike cigarettes. I was shocked, since I had never known him to smoke. I suspected that the Army had reduced him to that and heaven knows what else, so I dutifully collected all the cartons of Lucky Strikes I could, through swaps and buys, and sent them to him at his Army Post Office number. Later, when he came to visit me in Paris, he said he couldn't believe how dense I was: He never did smoke, but was trying to tell me in code that he was at Camp Lucky Strike, one of the receiving camps – named after cigarettes – for newly arrived GIs in Europe.

On his first visit to Paris, Irv. went to the Red Cross Hotel and looked me up on the register. He found a Melvin Corren, but when he went to the listed address, it wasn't me. Not one to give up, he went back and searched again. This time he found the real me and went to my billet. I was out at the time so he plopped himself down on my cot and took a nap.

When I returned, I was, of course, surprised to see him in my bed, but not wanting to waste a minute, got him up and took him out on the town.

Our first destination was to the famous American Bar near the Bastille. It was run by an ex Yankee left over from World War I. Being the only GIs in the place that night, we were celebrities. Everyone wanted to buy us a drink. Irv, who not only didn't smoke but was unaccustomed to drinking hard liquor, chose Manhattans because they tasted so sweet. We had them lined up and drank them quickly in order to go on to the GI cabaret, where we got a table, two dancing partners and a bottle of champagne. After toasting one another, we escorted our two lovelies on to the dance floor, where we proceeded to trip the light fantastic. However, a few minutes later, when I looked around to see where Irv and his partner were, I spotted him alone at the table with his face in the plate.

I got him to his feet and out on the sidewalk, and began walking him back to my place in the direction of the Etoile when a couple of French *pompiers* (firemen) came along. Noting Irv's condition, they hoisted him between them and walked with us all the way back to my billet, to the beat of Irv's constant exclamation, "Booooy. These guys are really great!"

This is the only time we went "out on the town" and in future years he would complain that on his visits to Paris I took him only to the museums and not to the likes of the Follies Bergere.

As I previously mentioned, none of the GIs who visited me believed that the cafes on the Champs Elysees really served as our mess halls. When I took them there for meals, they assumed I was treating them.

Even more unbelievable is that when Bob and I chose not to eat at

these mess halls, we ate in the chef's, invitation-only, dining room in the basement of the Majestic Hotel (the hotel was the headquarters of our commanding general, and later the site of the signing of the treaty that ended the Vietnam War). Bob and I had an ongoing invitation to eat there at the long table where the French chef held court. Our invitation was a perk our commanding officer arranged with one of his counterparts. I suppose you might call it quid pro something or other.

It was there that I had a very close encounter with a general. We had just finished eating breakfast at the Majestic, and Bob and I were about to go our separate ways when we ran

smack into our general and his entourage.

I was dressed casually that morning, my tie hanging from unbuttoned collar, as I had the weekend off and was on my way to visit my Uncle Al in Rheims. The general stopped short and, in a commanding voice, asked, "What's wrong with this picture, soldier?"

Bob, an amateur photographer and later a professional one, looked around and asked, "Picture, what picture?" in his decidedly New York twang. Whereupon the General stepped in front of me, cinched up my tie, and returned my salute, exclaiming, "Now you look like a soldier!"

As I recall, this was the same general whose headquarters initially insisted we stand reveille at 6 a.m. In the courtyards and streets of Paris. Our voices would reverberate, prompting sleep-deprived Parisians to complain to the American military government. Fortunately, after a week or so, reveille was discontinued.

I have already mentioned that my dad had many friends in the furniture business who were traveling salesmen and would, when stopping over in Stockton, be invited to our house for dinner. One of these men wrote to me while I was in Paris and asked me to visit his grandfather who was living in a convalescent hospital on the outskirts of the city. It wasn't a very pleasant place, still, I couldn't understand how this old Jewish man was able to live in this facility when other Jews of Paris were being taken away to concentration camps.

CAMP KILMER EXCHANGE
CAMP KILMER, NEW BRUNSWICK, N. J.
TELEPHONE: NEW BRUNSWICK 8100

ALR:jh

CKCG

17 January 1946

Pfc. Melvin H. Corren, 19190349
c/o M. Corren and Sons
136 South San Joaquin St.
Stockton, California

Dear Private Corren:

     Via parcel post, we have this day forwarded to you a wallet which is apparently your property and which was found in one of the branches of this Exchange.

     We obtained your home address thru Mr. Henry Brandler, with whom you apparently had correspondence, and which was the quickest means of locating you, after an examination of the contents of this wallet.

     The wallet is being returned with the contents intact, as submitted to this office.

Yours very truly,

ALFRED L. RANDALL
Captain, T. C.
Chief, Army Exchange Branch

I received the above letter when I returned home, along with a package containing the wallet I lost at Camp Kilmer. As the letter states, it was able to be returned to me because of the return address on the letter in which the man asked me to visit his grandfather.

Yet another coincidence.

PHOTOS:

Irv and me with another famous fixture in Paris, a photo by a friend.
A recent photo I took of a similar "Mess hall" as ours on the Champs Elysees

Paradise Lost... Almost

At one point, the real war nearly caught up with me. It was during the Battle of the Bulge, which began on December 17, 1944, when the U.S. Army was cut off during a desperate counterattack by the German army near Bastogne. This was to be the last-ditch battle by the Nazis in France.

Although American forces were badly outnumbered, the commanding general, Brigadier General Anthony C. McAuliffe, famously responded to the German demand for surrender with the single word reply, "Nuts!". (a bit of American slang that proved a puzzlement for the Germans).

The GIs held out against overwhelming odds in one of the costliest and most heroic battles of the war. They finally broke through, but before the breakthrough, the situation was tenuous, and it looked as though the enemy and the cold might ultimately win out. There were nearly as many casualties from frostbite as from enemy action. It was also discovered that 84 GI prisoners of war were disarmed and summarily executed in a field.

Here's how I came into the equation: The closest replacements were the headquarter troops in Paris, and the plan was to send those of us who were physically capable to the front. All personnel in the Com Z, S.O.S. Seine Section were ordered to report for a physical exam.

The call-up was alphabetical, starting from A to G. This placed me in the first group and I, once again, gave away my garrison equipment in view of my probable future.

I speculated that because of all the many times I had heard the phrase "kill or be killed," my odds were, by definition, short.

When the orders were published I couldn't believe my name was not on the list. Since then, when I read accounts or see movies about that horrific battle, I wonder, to this day, had I been selected would I have survived and, if so, would the horrors I'd have most probably seen haunt me for the rest of my life in the form of Post-Traumatic Stress Disorder?

May 8, 1945: VICTORY IN EUROPE!

We, the military and civilian population in Paris, waited virtually in safety while the real heroes, the combat soldiers, made it possible for us to finally celebrate V.E. (Victory in Europe) Day, on May 8th, 1945. It was a day to remember. People poured into the streets by the thousands, dancing, kissing, drinking, eating and parading.

Although the celebration continued for several days, the most impressive thing for me that night occurred on the terrace

of the Trocadero. My friends and I were looking out to the Eiffel Tower across the river at the very moment that it, along with the other famous monuments in the city, were lit up after those four ugly and degrading years of darkness – a darkness that encompassed more than just the extinguishing of the lights.

I went to celebrate with my French friends who lived within walking distance of my billet and when I arrived I found the woman of the house crying uncontrollably. I couldn't believe my eyes. When I finally got her to listen, I asked her why she was crying on this most wonderful day. She answered, "You Americans are so naive, now you will be fighting the Russians."

How prophetic!

Later, when we joined the crowd on the plaza of the Trocadero, overlooking the Warsaw Fountains, we looked out on the Eiffel Tower, again bathed in light. I went back to Avenue d'Iena later that night and celebrated again with Bob and my fellow soldiers as we speculated on how long we would remain in this magnificent city.

The next day, at our depot on rue Fresnel, the mood was relaxed except for much speculation as to the rotation of troops.

The word was out that we would be going home for a furlough and then to the C.B.I.: China, Burma, India Theater of Operations to participate in the Japanese invasion.

However, due to the atomic bombing, and

subsequent defeat of Japan, we had to sweat out the point system which determined when we, as individuals, could return home.

It worked like this: We were given points for our time in the service, time spent overseas, time in combat and other accomplishments. When the number added up to the required total we were ready to ship home and be discharged.

For those who didn't have enough points to go right home, the army arranged a week or 10 day leave to specified places in Europe. I wanted to go with an Italian soldier friend to Italy, but was denied because food was scarce, and only soldiers with relatives in that country could go there.

I chose instead to go to Switzerland and had a wonderful tour of a European country that had remained neutral and seemed not to be touched by the war. There were several of us on that trip and during our train tour through practically the whole country the Swiss treated us very well.

We heard of many reasons why Switzerland was designated to be neutral during the war, but the best ones were the ones we heard from some of the older men who said that Germany decided to make the country neutral because they couldn't beat the Swiss in the mountains.

I heard this on one occasion in a bar when a man told the story with an old blunderbuss hanging from his arm.

My cousin, Irv. had the same opportunity after the war but, since he was a serious musician, decided to go to a music school which was offered in England. There he studied piano with another G.I., Dave Brubeck, after which, although Irv. was very talented, he decided to study law when he got home.

When I returned from Switzerland I had nearly enough points to go home, but was offered a job with the Army to be part of a cadre opening the university for occupation troops in Biarritz. I considered it, but I and my folks wanted me to come home.

And so I did.

PHOTOS:

Photo of the Victory in Europe parade on the Champs Elysees. (My photo)

Photo of a group of the guys and gals in ComZ in front of the depot on rue Fresnel, Paris. Bob and I are not in the picture. We must have been on an adventure. (Photographer unknown)

Note: To learn about the Biarritz University, google U.S. Army university at Biarritz, France.

Returning Home

The last and most bizarre coincidence occurred the day I left Avenue d'iena for a staging area on the outskirts of Paris, on the way to Le Havre and the ship that would take me home.

I arrived at the staging area, but had forgotten something at Avenue d'Iena, so I picked up the phone to call Bob Rieders. The person who answered yelled something like, "Rieders, Corren is on the phone for you." My cousin Irv., who was traveling through Paris and did not know that I was on my way home, had just walked in the door, and when he heard that yell, he

found Bob and spoke to me on the phone. We set up a meeting and got together for a last visit in Europe. For the last time, I passed on my garrison equipment – this time to my cousin, who was staying on for a little while longer.

Yes, I was on my way home. The group I sailed home with was a collection of soldiers who were, for the most part, only acquaintances and who didn't become very well connected during the time it took to assemble in Le Havre and cross the ocean aboard the USS Mount Vernon. However, we melded into a sentimental unit on that

memorable moment when we passed the Statue of Liberty.

We were standing on deck, and the first one to spot the Lady in the harbor let out a yell and we broke into song. We sang at the top of our lungs some of the songs dedicated to the country we had spent the last years and months serving. At least one of the songs was composed by Irving Berlin, the man who my grandmother had claimed to be a relative. It was a highly emotional moment and I don't think even the most callous of us had a dry eye. Another unforgettable experience to add to all those we had already lived through. It was short lived, however, as after that tearful moment, we set our sights on going to wherever we called home, that unique place in America.

First, though, I had to fulfill my promise to Bob to visit his parents so after I got off the ship and settled in at camp, I called the number he had given me and arranged to dine with them in their apartment in Washington Heights. I made the date for 7 p.m., but didn't arrive until about 9 because I hadn't realized how long it would take to go through the Lincoln Tunnel and locate their apartment building – which occupied a solid block.

It was good to talk with them about Bob and me.

The next morning I boarded a plane for my second-ever airplane ride, from New Jersey to Sacramento, where I was discharged at Camp Beale and sent home to Stockton. Home Sweet Home!

POST SCRIPT:

At this point, I must confess to a couple of things which have been on my mind for lo these many years:

First: After the war, except for a brief period of correspondence during which I sent clothing and other items, I dropped the ball with the families who had been so hospitable to me while I was overseas. It wasn't until my mother took Harriet and me on our first trip to England and France in 1969 that I was able to renew our friendships. I reunited with all but one family, the Bouyers, whose last letter from me, as previously stated, was returned with the stamp, "Décède".

Second: The pang of guilt I feel when I say, "I can't imagine a more rewarding experience while serving my country."

To assuage that guilt I remind myself that we who served behind the lines were just youngsters, away from home and family, doing what we were assigned. It was just exceptionally good luck that some of us won the mega prize in what must have been the deadliest lottery of all time.

PHOTOS:

At La Havre-ready to board ship

Cousin Irv in my Garrison Cap I gave him the day I left Paris

Passing the Statue of Liberty coming in to NY Harbor. (My photo)

Home Again

When I arrived home, I found that so much had changed – including myself – that it was difficult to get back into the swing of things. For almost a year I was hard to live with. As my family has reminded me, I found fault with many ordinary things. It was a depressing time for me. Everything was, or seemed to be, so much different from what I had known it to be.

For example, my family's form of Judaism before I went into the Army had been quasi orthodox in the *shul*. When I returned, it had become more reform. Our family had always belonged to both congregations and I was familiar with both, but it was still difficult at first to accept the reform, which I had in the past associated with Sunday school This change in religious direction was traumatic at first, but in time I began to prefer the reform to the orthodox, since I could understand what I was reading (in the orthodox we had been taught only to *read* Hebrew, but not understand it). Our whole family then got involved in the temple and ultimately became leaders, producing four presidents: my dad, Sam; my brother, Hillard; my wife, Harriet (the first woman to hold that position); and our cousin, Craig. In addition, many of us have been board members, including me, and have served the temple in many ways.

Cpl. Melvin H. Corren, son of Mr. and Mrs. Sam Corren, 2255 Lakeside, has been honorably discharged from the Army after three years' service. Entering the Army in November, 1942, Cpl. Corren was assigned to the Army Service CORREN Forces and was sent overseas in October, 1943, with the Headquarters Command Theater of Operations. A supply clerk, Cpl. Corren has been awarded the European Theater Ribbon with two battle stars and the Victory Medal

Rabbi Levy was the reform rabbi when I attended Sunday school and during WWII he served as a chaplain. Rabbi Rosenberg was the rabbi when both our sons, Howard and Donald, were Bar Mitzvahed and merged the services a little closer to the Conservative style. Rabbi Steven Chester, who married Howard and Marty, was the rabbi when my wife, Harriet, was the first woman president of the congregation. Later, a precedent was set when Rabbi Selig Salkowitz served us as a one year interim rabbi between rabbis. He was the first rabbi to serve as such, however, it is now a regular position in the Reform Movement.

Our present rabbi, Jason Gwasdoff, has innovated many family and social programs that have made the congregation very friendly to the children as well as to the community at large. His wife, Lindy Passer, is the cantorial soloist and conducts a congregational choir (*kolot*), in which I've sung until recently.

There were changes in the family business, as well. Shortly after the war Miss Shrieky, the landlady of M. Corren and Sons, passed away. This meant the family was able to buy the furniture store, as well as a new store right next door, separated by a sizable parking lot. This new store featured the full array of modern household appliances, including electric clothes dryers, dishwashers, garbage disposals, automatic ovens, and all the other postwar innovations that soon became a standard part of our home furnishings inventory.

The main store was remodeled and greatly modernized. The upper floor, originally a narrow balcony on four sides of a mezzanine, was bridged over, creating a genuine second floor. A large display window in the front was reconstructed as a radio broadcasting studio, which broadcast the M. Corren and Sons "Friendly Furniture Hour". This program consisted of interviews, discussions, music and, of course, advertising. Ahead of its time, what?

A warehouse was created above the new Appliance Store in a space which, until then, had been a "house that was not a home" – that is to say, a house of ill-repute. (I can now admit, after all these years, that when I was working in this upstairs warehouse, I would occasionally listen to the walls, hoping to hear a few titillating snips of conversation., but I heard nothing....not even "Never More").

Stockton had been a "closed" town in so far as gambling and prostitution were concerned, but that was only on paper. In reality the town was "quasi open". Prostitution was a controlled and supervised business, with the proper medical supervision and inspection. This made it a service to the city, as the area housed a large number of single men who picked the crops and had no ties to women in the community.

Gambling houses flourished in "China Town" on Washington Street just southwest of our family's furniture store. This China Town was noted to be the third largest in Northern California and a major attraction for the city of Stockton, as it was considered one of the most colorful ones in the country.

The most popular games were "Black Jack", "Chuck a Luck" (a kind of lottery) and "Fan Tan".

One would often hear the melodious call, "Twaaanty One!" ringing through the room when someone got a Black Jack or hit to 21.

People came from far and near to eat at On Lock Sam's, The King Cafe, Canton Low, and many other locally owned Chinese Restaurants in what was then such a colorful and thriving neighborhood. This was also true of other local restaurants such The Pioneer Tamale House, The El Kobar and El Tehran. There was even a Chinese Cabaret on Weber Avenue called "The Golden Dragon" in which, as has already been mentioned, Irv and I took piano lessons right up on stage.

I and so many of my contemporaries often reminisced about walking up the stairs of On Lock Sam's Restaurant, being greeted by a member of the Wong family, and entering a booth where, behind a closed curtain, we were served the most delicious dishes.

When we kids went with our dad he would head straight for the kitchen, where he would buy all the cooks a drink while helping himself to the tasty bits and pieces they offered him. We couldn't wait until we got old enough to accompany him. Years later, after redevelopment and construction of the Cross Town Freeway, China Town was relocated, but having lost its authenticity it lost its allure.

At this juncture, it would be well to mention a few things that over the years became great matters of consternation for the Corren family business: In the early 1920s, my dad made what was probably the largest contract of his life to that date. It was the selling and installing of cork flooring, a fairly new product from the Armstrong Cork Company, in a very large public building. This was a very exciting event, of course, but the day the installation was finished, the building's architect sent for my dad to point out that the specs called for *sanded* cork. My dad knew nothing about cork being sanded and it cost the fledgling business money it could ill afford.

In the years after World War II, the downtown area changed dramatically. Once a thriving, vital center of commerce, where men and women were for the most part well-dressed (my mother often recalled that women wore hats and gloves), the downtown became less important as other business centers sprouted up north of town. Some worked to reverse the slide, but the large shopping malls and strip centers in the north ultimately forced the downtown merchants out of the neglected center. This also gradually changed the Miracle Mile on Pacific Avenue from a chic neighborhood shopping center to an also-ran which has, happily, come back in recent years.

M. Corren and Sons was located on South San Joaquin Street, across from the East side of St. Mary's Catholic Church, and because the church was more interested in benefiting mankind than the business climate it set up a dining hall, staffed by volunteers who fed the poor. This was frowned on by many of the downtown merchants as it attracted long lines of down-and-out folks, right in the heart of the business district. The long line, predominantly men in those days, affected mostly the Correns' store, so some urged the Corren brothers to go before the city council to protest. Due to their principles and the teachings of their parents, they refused, even though it might have been better for their business. Today in a different location this dining hall is a respected member of the community.

Another traumatizing event for the Correns occurred when the Crosstown freeway was conceived and then constructed on Washington Street. It became a veritable barrier on the Southside of the store as well as a separation of the North and South sides of Stockton's downtown.

Had it not been for Ort Loftus who fought for it's completion, and for whom the Freeway is named, it would not have served as the connector of Highways 5 and 99 as planned, but would have remained the "Freeway merely to Stanislaus Street", where it had ended for some time before he saw to its completion.

The Correns' sold the store in 1978 to a company which then ran a huge going out of business sale under a very large banner headline.

The irony of this was that the family had always prided itself on never having run a sale. The following headlines tell the story:

A few years later the new owners sold the property to make room for the San Joaquin County Human Services Agency building which now occupies the site.

PHOTOS:

Newspaper article announcing my homecoming (Stockton Record article)

1964 headline reprinted with permission of Home Furnishings News

1978 headline reprinted courtesy of Record newspaper, Stockton, CA.

MEL CORREN

Ongoing Friendships

Bob Rieders was the fellow soldier I had the most in common with during my stint in the Army and the only one I kept in touch with over the past 70 plus years. We first met in Valognes, Normandy, before reuniting a few days later in Paris, where we spent nearly a year and a half working together, playing together and seeing the sights of the city – not at all bad duty.

Shortly after we returned to civilian life, Bob and three of his friends drove out from

New York City to visit me in California. After that Bob moved to St. Louis, Mo. and we lost touch for several years. Then, by chance, a friend of mine from the old days

on Walnut Street, Marlene Belew Hnath, had photos taken of her children in St. Louis by a photographer, Bob Rieders, who, when she mentioned she was returning to Stockton, asked if she knew Mel Corren. When she answered yes, he told her our story and that's how Bob and I got back together.

Bob and his wife, Elaine, both of whom have since passed on, moved to a beautiful retirement community, The Gatesworth, which is best described as an eternal cruise in premier class.

Since Bob was involved for many years in the St. Louis Jazz scene he was able to bring in groups to entertain. This made him popular with both the residents and the staff.

During our stays with him we were treated like VIPs and driven around town in a chauffeured limousine!

Along with Bob and Elaine Rieders and family, Harriet and I have kept in touch –

following a lapse of many years – with other families I met overseas.

We have visited with them in England and France, celebrated Weddings, Anniversaries, Bat Mitzvahs and other celebrations in both countries.

In addition to our visits, all of ours and their children and grandchildren have done likewise.

§

The fact that I was able to see another part of the world while serving my time in the Army made all the difference in my life, and I'm keenly aware and grateful for my good fortune to have been in the right place at the right time when good things came my way.

And, being stationed in Paris for very nearly a year and a half gave me something I would never have had otherwise. For, as Ernest Hemingway wrote: "If you are lucky enough to have lived in Paris as a young man, then wherever you go for the rest of your life, it stays with you, for Paris is a moveable feast."

It is so true because when you meet someone with that same experience it is the opening for a nostalgic conversation.

PHOTOS:

Bob Rieders and me

Bob and his friends visiting from New York

Harriet and me with Bob and Elaine Rieders

Harriet with Laurence, J.P. and Frederic in the Pithoud's living room

My grandson, Daniel, and his wife, Jen, Celine (center, Janine's grand daughter), Harriet and me

Anita and Gerry and their family when we visited them on their 50th wedding anniversary in London

Life Begins in Earnest

They say things happen for the best and they certainly did for me the day Miss Spalteholtz, my art teacher at Stockton Junior College, told me that if I wanted to be an interior decorator, I should look into a school in San Francisco. This school, named after its founder, was the Rudolph Schaefer School of Design that specialized in interior, floral and dress design. Several years later, just before the school closed, we celebrated his hundredth birthday with a group of alumni in San Francisco.

Heeding her advice, in June of 1946, I went to Schaefer's to see about enrolling but, although the course seemed interesting, the next class started at a time that conflicted with my curriculum at the junior college, where I had my heart set on graduating with a two-year Associate of Arts degree. I was disappointed, but as is my usual response to a setback, I decided to make the best of it. I called my aunt, Sadie Michaels – my mother's sister who worked at Milan's Jewelry Store nearby – and invited her to dinner.

We went to John's Grill, an old San Francisco favorite, and after a lovely meal, she departed, leaving me with no plans for the rest of the evening. I had been invited to stay at my aunt Sadie Blumenthal's house in the Avenues, however, and remembered that her daughter, my cousin Elaine, wanted me to meet a girlfriend of hers who lived around the block.

Because Elaine had arranged for cousin Irving to meet Ruthie, a beautiful girl he was planning to marry, I called her to ask if she would arrange for me to meet her other friend. She told me to wait at the public phone booth (no cell phones in those days), and she would call me back with an answer. I waited for what seemed like hours until she called with the good news that her friend would be awaiting our visit.

I hopped a streetcar, and as it was late by the time I arrived at Twenty-sixth Avenue, went promptly around the corner to meet – as it turned out – my destiny. We rang the bell at the entrance of a nice-looking apartment house and, upon being buzzed in, mounted the stairs to the apartment where I met my cousin Elaine's girlfriend, Harriet Berman.

The woman who answered the door was Harriet's mother. She was not thrilled with our arrival at that late hour since she had to awake at an early hour for work, but, after giving me the once-over – more than once – she called her daughter to the door.

I think I tried to be bright and engaging, but in reality I probably just stood there with my mouth agape. I hadn't expected to meet such a gorgeous girl.

After regaining my composure, I tried to make a good impression but it seemed a little strange that we were standing in the hallway. It was explained that it was a small apartment and the hour was late (8:30 p.m), so there I stood, amidst the mixture of odors given off by other

residents' cooking – doing my best to rise to the occasion. We invited Harriet to go out with us (Elaine, my brother Hillard, a sailor stationed at Treasure Island) and me. We received permission from Harriet's mother and the four of us went to a night club in San Francisco.

I thought myself to be quite classy in my brown flannel double breasted suit, necktie and V-neck sweater, but was later told that a sweater and tie was not very sophisticated. I assumed that I had made a rather dismal impression, but some 58

years later, Harriet confided in me that at our first meeting she knew I was the guy she would marry. You couldn't have proven it by me.

PHOTOS:

Class photo including Elaine, Irv's future wife, Ruthie, and my future wife, Harriet. (Photographer unknown)

Elian, Me and Hillard getting acquainted with Harriet. (Photographer unknown)

MEL CORREN

Harriet Berman Corren

Harriet's grandmother, Thelma, was married to Harry Verber, Harriet's grandfather, a part-time Hebrew teacher at Temple Beth Israel in San Francisco. Before that, in what must have seemed like another life, he had been a violinist and she a laundress who washed and ironed for the tsar's soldiers in Yakutsk, Siberia. We used to joke that he had "played fiddle for the tsar".

In 1904, during the height of the pogroms in Russia, the Verbers left Siberia, traveling overland to Vladivostok and on to Yokohama, where they stayed for five years before leaving for Seattle on the USS Minnesota. With them was their youngest daughter Lucille, born in Yakutsk in the late 1890s, who would, in the future, be Harriet's mother.

Other family members who immigrated include Thelma's sons, Abrasha and Leon, their daughter Ruth, and a half brother Mike, who was Thelma's son from another marriage.

Upon arriving in San Francisco, the Verbers were assisted by HIAS (The Hebrew Immigrant Aid Society), which, from the beginning of the Jewish emigration to America, saw to the newcomers' needs and began teaching them the American way of life, including the language.

Because she could count, Lucille went to work as a cash girl in a general store at a very early age. She married Harry Berman, son of Samuel and Rebecca Berman, who worked in a stock and bonds office and later became the owner/manager of the company.

After their marriage, the Bermans moved to an apartment at Seventeenth and California, later to 24th Ave, and finally to a large flat on 31st Avenue, in the Richmond district, near the beach. According to Lucille, that apartment had the first dishwasher in San Francisco and was furnished by the prestigious W&J Sloane Furniture Company.

All went well until Harry suffered a heart attack at age 31 and, ironically, at the Stanford University hospital, the most prestigious on the coast, he was treated with bed rest. This was the exact opposite of what is prescribed today. He was confined to his bed on and off for four years and at the age of 35, on his way to what was to be his first day back at the office, he died on the streetcar. Harriet was nine and her brother, Ira, was six.

Those years spent in bed could have been a complete waste, but Harry made good use of the time. His mind was always active, and during this confinement he worked on a credit card system that he sold for the Union Oil Company.

I never knew him, of course, but have been told he was a dynamic person with immense drive. He was once described to me as "the smartest man I ever knew" by an intelligent and successful friend of my father's who had regularly played bridge with him in San Francisco.

Realizing that his life might be shortened by his heart condition, Harry made a contract with Union Oil to protect his wife after his death. It stipulated that she would continue drawing his salary for two years afterward. This money went for groceries and other necessities, and helped pay off the many bills that had accumulated during his illness.

Harry hadn't lost all his recently amassed wealth during the Depression, because, as a broker, he bought and sold for his clients and whether they made or lost money he received a commission. He tried to bail out many of his clients, for whom he felt somehow responsible and it was believed that this burden might have triggered the heart problem that eventually killed him.

After his death, Lucille was left with Harry's stocks and securities, but the prices were down on most of them, and some well-intentioned friends advised her to sell and buy others that ultimately proved worthless.

Having lost all, Lucille, with little formal education but deep determination, set out to raise her two children as a single mother.

A woman less interested in her children's welfare and more in her own comfort may have moved to a lower rent neighborhood, but not Lucille. She moved to a smaller, less expensive flat in the same area so her children could maintain the same friends as before.

She found a job at a jewelry store, where she worked during the children's early years. She later took jobs in shoe and department stores, working on her feet for long hours – which resulted in painful varicose veins.

She constantly bore in mind her husband's request that she not remarry; he wanted to protect his children from having to have a stepfather (he had had a stepmother). He also asked her to see that the children were brought up properly, with a good Jewish education. These were heavy responsibilities for a young widow, but she handled them admirably.

Lucille was a very good-looking woman with a figure to match and, although she occasionally dated men who pursued her, she had a phobia about the "authorities" discovering she was going out and taking her children away.

There was a man who she liked very much. He was a wealthy furrier who offered her a great life if she would marry him. However, he was several years older and, having already nursed a spouse until death, she declined the offer. He later married another woman and lived to a healthy old age. He stayed in touch, however, and was good to her and the children throughout his life.

Lucille continued to work six days a week until the unionization of retail clerks limited the work week to only five, plus overtime. Hard work and long hours made it possible for her to live up to her husband's decrees, the importance of which she realized in later years, albeit at the expense of her own pleasures.

On retiring she moved from "The Avenues" in San Francisco to San Mateo to be closer to her son and daughter-in-law. Due to Social Security and a WWI military pension from Harry's Naval service, she was able to maintain herself.

Being less than gregarious and not having any hobbies, Lucille did not adjust well to retirement, although for a time she did help her son Ira in his new business. She built her life even more so around her grandchildren, especially Lauren and Holli, Ira and Jackie's daughters.

When the children were young and needed babysitting and the like, it was a good life for her, but when the girls became more involved with their own friends and activities, Lucille's sphere of influence became much narrower. Her only pleasures were being invited to spend time with her family who, understandably, had acquired interests and activities which did not always include her.

After several years of quasi isolation, Lucille, on a visit to our house in Stockton, fell and broke her hip. That began a descent that led to a prolonged stay in a convalescent home and her eventual death.

Harriet's younger brother, Ira, went into the army just before we were married, and as a result of cousin Clarence (Bob) Rubenstein's advice, landed a job in Berlin as a broadcaster on the Armed Forces Network. I've never heard him broadcast, but

believe he would have gone far in communications on returning to civilian life. Instead, he went to college in San Francisco and began working in the jewelry and pawn business. He opened his own shop, "Bill's Loans" and later became a salesman for a famous watch company, and ultimately established his own jewelry manufacturing business.

Ira is married to the former Jackie Levy and they have two daughters, Lauren and Holli. Lauren is married to Billy Mac Hill, is a school teacher in Kentucky, and has a daughter, Sophie. Holli is the cantor soloist in congregation Har Hashem in Boulder, Colorado, where Holli and her partner, Marcia Cotlar, are raising their twin sons, Jaron and Seth.

PHOTOS:

Harry Berman, Harriet's father in the navy WWI. The only surviving picture of him available (Photographer unknown)

Lucille Berman, Harriet's mother (Photographer unknown)

Ira's store, "Bill's Loans" (author's photo)

Wooing

After our initial meeting, the next time I saw Harriet was a month later, when my cousin Leland Metzger gave a big Fourth of July party at his parents' home (they were conveniently gone for the weekend). He invited all of our AZA brothers and their girlfriends from Sacramento, Oakland and San Francisco.

I invited Harriet to the party, but since I believed her mother was not in the least impressed with me, I was almost sure she wouldn't allow her to come, but to my great surprise she did. (I learned later it was because Ruthie, Irving's girl friend, and cousin Elaine were also attending!) The pride I felt at having Harriet on my arm at that party continues to this day. It's even more thrilling when I'm waiting somewhere for her to meet me, and I see the faces of those near us when she walks up and gives me a hug. WOW!

The next time we got together was when Elaine called to tell me that Harriet had a date with another fellow. She suggested I hightail it to San Francisco to join her and Mervin Cohn, an old friend who had formerly lived just down the

street from Elaine and Harriet. They had discovered that Harriet and her date were going to a tea dance at the Palace Hotel. I heeded the summons, borrowed the family car and met Elaine and Mervin at Elaine's house. The three of us then went on to the Garden Room of the Palace Hotel, where we saw Harriet and her date sitting at a table for two. We entered the room nonchalantly and asked to be seated at a table nearby. A little later, I worked up the courage to ask Harriet for a dance. She accepted, and when I escorted her back to the table, I found Mervin leaning over Harriet's date, suggesting that they join us at our table, which they did.

Our next date was on Yom Kippur. Buddy and Florence called to say they were going to a favorite Chinese restaurant in San Francisco and would I like to call Harriet and join them. It was a little dicey to ask my folks on my first Yom Kippur at home if I could go to San Francisco, but we compromised: I stayed for the services and left with Bud and Florence immediately afterward, missing the *up-fast* (break-the-fast) dinner. Harriet hit it off with Buddy and Florence from the first egg roll. Buddy is now deceased, but Harriet and Florence – who is now Hillard's significant other (as the world turns) – have remained good friends.

From then on, Harriet and I were an Item. During our courtship, we spent almost every weekend together – in separate houses, of course. We covered all the night spots, and have the cabaret photos to prove it.

A few weeks later, we went to Joe Di Maggio's, a famous nightclub at Fisherman's Wharf, to see a floor show. There was a minimum cover charge, so before the show began, we all had a couple of drinks lined

up before us except for Harriet, who didn't drink anything but water in those days. The waiter tried to entice her to order something to satisfy the rule and suggested something sweet. When her "sweet" arrived, it turned out to be a large mixing bowl with mounds of delicious ice cream in different flavors. We all abandoned our drinks and dug into her trophy dessert.

Our group was large and close-knit and seemed to click on everything. We ranged in residence from the San Francisco Bay Area, including the Peninsula and Marin County, to Sacramento, and of course, Stockton.

Irv went to the University of San Francisco Law School and married Ruthie, the San Francisco girl cousin Elaine had introduced him to before he went in the Army.

Uncle Harry bought Irv a Ford convertible and he would drive Ruthie and Harriet to Stockton almost every weekend. They married before he finished law school and had two sons, Marc and Todd.

Sadly, after 27 years of wedded bliss, Ruthie passed away, which broke Irving up unbelievable. Several years later, he married Shirley, who has been a wonderful wife and helpmate to him. Shirley had worked for Irv as a legal secretary before they were married, and afterward worked for the state until retiring.

After graduating with a law degree and returning to Stockton, Irv started out in the district attorney's office. He then went into practice with a well-established firm, and from there went out on his own to develop a superb reputation as a defense attorney. He practiced for approximately 45 years before retiring, but just before he died, the San Joaquin County Bar Association named him Lawyer of the Year in 2004 and honored him at a law day celebration, during which a conference room was named in his honor.

I had just given my fraternity pin to Harriet and couldn't wait to show her off to my school friends. So, when the 1946 Mardi Gras, the most elaborate dance of the year at the College of the Pacific came around, it was the perfect opportunity to do just that.

I can't remember the costumes the rest of us wore, but I do remember buying Harriet a suede cowgirl vest with leather fringes at Mrs. Stone's used clothing store, which in those days was the headquarters for costuming in Stockton. She kept the vest for many years, but never wore it again.

After keeping company (or "going steady," as it was called in those days) for several months, Harriet and I announced our engagement during my parents' 25th Wedding anniversary.

My dad bought us a Plymouth coupe when we became engaged. It was robin-egg blue and sported every gizmo available at the time. The beautiful grey plush mohair seats, which molded to the body, along with the especially soft ride made it a very comfortable car. It seems nowadays it's desirable to "feel the road".

PHOTOS:

Harriet and me when we were dating

Irv and Ruthie, Hillard and Libby, and Harriet and me in Irv's Ford convertible

Harriet, Libby and Ruthie

Mother and Dad's 25th anniversary: Me, mom, dad, Doralee and Hillard (Our engagement was announced after the toasts were made and the anniversary cake was cut.)

Harriet in front of our first car

MEL CORREN

Wedded Bliss

After months of planning, our wedding day - October 11, 1947 – finally arrived and I found myself sitting in Rabbi Bernstein's study in the Geary Street Temple, anxiously awaiting the wedding ceremony to begin. I wasn't exactly nervous, but I do remember signing papers that were legal and binding *'till death do us part!* It just seems that they could come up with a phrase more conducive to the joy of the event.

Although Harriet belonged to the California Street Temple, we couldn't serve champagne there, and it didn't have a room large enough to accommodate Harriet's large family plus the equally large one into which she was marrying. So we were married instead on Geary Street (in the same building that later became the infamous People's Temple), with two rabbis officiating. Many of our relatives

Mrs. Lucille Berman
requests the honor of your presence
at the marriage of her daughter
Harriet
to
Mr. Melvin Herschel Corren
on Saturday evening, the eleventh of October
at half after eight o'clock
Congregation Beth Israel
Eighteen thirty-nine Geary Street
San Francisco

Mr. and Mrs. Melvin Corren
The former Harriet Berman and her husband will return to a home in Stockton from a southern California trip. (du Charme Photo)

and friends were doing the same thing at about the same time, and we all took part in each other's ceremonies. Our weddings were very much alike, but we each planned our own distinctive honeymoons – except for one thing: We all stayed at least one night at the Chapman Park Hotel in Los Angeles.

Our wedding was beautifully planned by Harriet's mother and went off very well except for the fact that one important person was missing: Ira, the bride's brother, was in Berlin as a member of the occupation army, working as a disc jockey announcer with the Armed Forces Network. He was sorely missed, but as we have come to realize in our show biz family, "The show must go on."

In preparation for the occasion, my folks arranged for me to have "the works" at the hotel barbershop. While the barber was cutting my hair, the manicurist, being a little talkative, asked why I was getting a manicure since I guess my nails didn't look that pampered. I told her about my upcoming wedding, and she asked who I was marrying. I told her it was Harriet Berman, and she asked if she was Harry Berman's daughter. When I answered yes, she told me she had given him a manicure every week in that very shop at that very chair. She also mentioned what a wonderful gentleman he was, a coincidence that made it seem fate was intervening from the other side.

Uncle Willie Berman, Harriet's father's brother, bought the license and gave Harriet away. I kiddingly remind Harriet that Uncle Willie bought her for me, which goes over like a lead balloon.

Du Charme Studios took many photos for our wedding book and I liked them all with the exception

of one. I told my new mother-in-law I didn't think that picture was suitable because I looked like a ventriloquist's dummy, dressed in a tuxedo and standing alongside my bride with her long train cascading down the stairs. She told me that since she had bought the gown and paid for the pictures, the photo was not only going to be included in the album, but would be made into the framed 8 x 10 which has, for all these years, hung in our hallway.

In spite of that, you had to hand it to my mother-in-law, Lucille. Despite her limited income, she not only bought the most beautiful wedding dress and trousseau for Harriet that anyone of greater means could have found, but during the early years of our marriage when we needed help, she sent us both beautiful clothes from the first pickings off sale racks at whichever of the fine stores she was working. She continued to do this throughout our children's growing-up period. Ira would drive her to Stockton almost every weekend with clothes for us and the children. It was on these visits that Uncle Ira became the great mentor he was to Howard and Donald.

§

The ceremony and the reception at the Geary Street Temple (later the infamous Jim Jone's Peoples Temple) went off beautifully and we finally got away to our first-night hotel, the Claremont in Berkeley. It was a very fashionable place, as it still is.

When we arrived at the front desk with rice in our hair, a bellhop showed us to our room, which had a lovely view of the Bay and as a means of making us feel welcome, the bellman, who was Filipino, asked where we were from. I told him I was from Stockton, and he started talking about the days he spent in the area's asparagus fields. It seemed to go on for hours, but finally he was gone and we were alone in our hotel room.

You have to remember that it wasn't then as it is now. I couldn't get over the fact that a signature, a couple of pieces of paper and some words from the rabbi could make it all right for us to be in the same hotel room. (Anyone born after the 1960s is probably laughing out loud while reading this.)

The next day we drove to Los Angeles, where we stayed at the Chapman Park Hotel. We were entertained by Harriet's cousin, Walter Shenson, who was a publicity man at one of the studios and later became a famous producer of Peter Sellers and the Beatles movies. He seemed to know all the Stars at the famous Brown Derby restaurant so it made for a very exciting evening.

We heard Sophie Tucker sing at the Florentine Gardens and bought her book, *Some of these Days*. Cousin Ida Sherman, a telephone operator in Hollywood, got us the tickets, which were hard to come by. Ida was not only a telephone operator, a "number please" kind as they were in those days, but also a regular wheeler-dealer in the entertainment community. She was the first person I really knew who was connected with show business. She wasn't a singer, actor or any other kind of person in the trade, but she made it her business to know everyone in those circles, and as a telephone operator in a time before press-one-for-whatever superseded personal contact, she was in the know.

Returning to our honeymoon: We drove down to Wilmington to board a ship for the big Island – Catalina that is. It was very quiet there in October, but we didn't mind. It gave us a little down time to get better acquainted.

It was on the boat heading back to the mainland that Harriet got to know the real me. I was sitting on a bench aboard ship, minding my own business, when suddenly I felt my legs go to sleep, which meant I couldn't get up. Having a vivid imagination and relating the numbness to the most feared malady of the time, I announced to my bride of less than a week that I had probably contracted polio. Though taken aback, Harriet quickly realized my panic was unfounded, and, in the ensuing years, has gracefully put up with my periodic bouts of hypochondria.

I'm happy to say that it's been over sixty-eight years since that first trip and we've enjoyed many wonderful ones since.

PHOTOS:

Our wedding invitation
A photo article from a San Francisco newspaper
The wedding party: Uncle Willie, Lucille, Harriet, me, mom and dad.
The Bride and Groom
Harriet on Catalina Island on our Honeymoon...
...and returning on the boat from Catalina

Building a Nest

Our honeymoon flew by and we headed back to Stockton, where we had one side of a duplex waiting for us to begin our wedded life. This duplex belonged to my uncle Maurice Corren; he lived in the adjoining side. We furnished ours in American Colonial, complete with a Duncan Pfyfe-style sofa and dining set to match. The furnishings were a gift from my father and uncles. They allowed us to pick furniture from their store as a wedding present from the family. It was a very generous gift, and the fact that each of us cousins received an equivalent wedding gift was even more so.

We had begun to settle in and everything seemed to be going along swimmingly when it happened: I arrived home from work one evening, thinking it had been a day like any other and found the dining table set with our new china and silver along with a centerpiece of flowers. I innocently asked Harriet who was coming for dinner and was answered with tears, sobs and the first flush of recrimination in our new home. It seems it was the four-month anniversary of our married life, and I was supposed to be as excited

about it as she was. I guess I had been planning on a little more longevity before celebrating.

Many things happened in our first home which have stayed in our memories, some of them even eclipsing my fourth-month anniversary gaffe. Uncle Maurice and Aunt Sophie, our landlords, bought the first TV set in the family at the same time our son Howard was born. It was a round Zenith 12-inch screen. It commanded almost as much attention as our firstborn, who was also a little round. Company arrived for quite awhile to see the two firsts in the same location. It was great because it gave us the opportunity to show off our firstborn to the whole family at once.

The duplex was just a couple of blocks from where I had spent my preadolescent years, so I was well acquainted with the neighborhood. Everything was new for Harriet but she, being who she is, made friends easily and entered into temple life where she made her mark as president of the sisterhood and later the first female president of the temple. The neighborhood offered a great deal for a young family. There were two groceries, a five-and-dime store, a hardware store, a Chinese restaurant, three wonderful creameries, a movie theater and several clothing stores. Later, when we moved to our present home across the street from the Lincoln Village Shopping Center, we were fortunate to have access to similar shops.

Our years in the duplex gave us a wonderful start. We were able to come and go as we pleased, because babysitters were never for away, with Uncle Maurice, Auntie Sophie and their son Leonard living next to us.

Many people helped us in those early years. Sam Ferdman, Libby's father, and Jake Cooper, Aunt Gertrude's father, painted and papered the nursery in preparation for Howard's arrival. I wonder if we appreciated it enough at the time.

Around the corner on Pacific Avenue was the Dubois Dress Shop which helped me make the first and greatest hit of my entire married life. It was Valentine's Day, and I saw this bright red corduroy suit in the window. What could be more apropos? I bought it, had it wrapped appropriately, bought a valentine, walked around the corner and presented it to my bride. Harriet was so impressed that she has never stopped talking about it. Every Valentine's Day, or whenever we see a red outfit in a store window, she recalls how thrilled she was to receive that first Valentine's gift as a married woman.

Our side of the duplex which was on Concord Street at the corner of Walnut was on the beaten path, and years later we learned that on Sunday mornings, when Howard was seen in his play pen on the lawn outside (that could be done in those days), there was speculation as to where we might be.

Professor Irving Goleman and his family lived across the street from us. His class, "World Literature, the Autobiography of Civilization" at Stockton Junior College, was the most memorable of my entire educational career.

The following is an excerpt of what I wrote while away in the Army:

Do you remember Professor Irving Goleman? Ask that of anyone who ever had Professor Goleman as a mentor, and he or she will tell you that it is absolutely impossible to forget him.

I can still see those handsome features, those full and eyebrows and that full mustache slightly covering those sharp white teeth. I can still hear somewhere inside my head those words of wisdom which he hammered out in that unique, pleading growl—each word biting into my very being. He lectured to the entire class, but somehow, it seemed the words he spoke were meant for me alone.

Do I remember Irving Goleman? Is it possible to forget someone who is somehow a part of you? For as he constantly reminded us that, "We are the sum total of our past," and, as a result of those few words, I and many others have been especially aware that we should add in some positive way to the heritage which was passed on to us.

I do remember Professor Irving Goleman, vividly, because he was the one person, who, outside of my family, had the most influence on the way I have tried to live my life.

His widow, Fay Goleman, a dear friend of mine, was a Professor Emerita at the University of the Pacific. I can still visualize her coming from Pacific Avenue down South Central Court in her Plymouth coupe, or walking, complete with her trademark knitted beret, and stopping off at our store for a little chit chat.

§

While we were still childless, I used my GI Loan to attend the Rudolph Schaefer School in San Francisco – the one I had attempted to

enroll in the day I met Harriet. (One month, I received two GI checks, which I cashed, thinking I had outwitted Uncle Sam. A few months later, I received a bill for the $65 plus interest. That taught me not to fool around with the government.)

I worked in the family store on Tuesday, Wednesday and Saturday. On Monday, Thursday and Friday, I went to school. On those days, we would sleep overnight at Auntie Sadie and Uncle Ernest's

house. We've always supposed that Howard began his embryonic life on one of those sleepovers.

All went well during that work-and-school period until the very last day, when I came down with violent cramps and fainted at the school. They took me upstairs, laid me out on a couch and called Auntie Sadie's house. Harriet got the call and immediately contacted Irv, who was attending the University of San Francisco. He picked her up and the two of them came down to get me.

I was taken to my mother-in-law's doctor who suggested I go straight to the hospital. I refused, saying that I was OK to go back to Stockton and see my own doctor, who happened to be our best friend, Hal Berkman. Hal ran some tests and diagnosed a duodenal inflammation, which he told me could become an ulcer. He prescribed some medication, and I asked him what more I could do to prevent a recurrence. He told me to think up through my head instead of down into my stomach. This advice helped tremendously, and I never suffered from that kind of pain again. I often applauded him for his brilliance, and he replied "Did I say that?"

§

My dad was very involved in the politics of the furniture business, having been the regional president of the Association at one time. One Market Week, when they were planning a forum to discuss the pros and cons of extending easy credit to customers (the no-down-payment craze was just beginning), he volunteered me as one of the speakers. I was about 25 years old and all the other speakers were considerably older, but I gave it a college try.

§

It was while doing the interior decorating at the store that I came up with the idea that if I could lay out a plan and sell the basic pieces of furniture to furnish a room, I could then, on delivery, take along several choices of lamps, pictures and accessories to compliment the setting. In this way we could set up the entire room in one fell swoop. This allowed our customers to enjoy the finished product while their interest was piqued and their inclination to enjoy and show off the new creation was strongest. This modus operandi worked beautifully for both the customer and the store. Years later at The Brothers, it was the only way we delivered merchandise: We'd wait until all the basic pieces arrived and then accompany the delivery with the "Goody Truck" which was loaded with complimenting accessories. It was a stratagem which worked in two ways: After the plan was sold and the merchandise ordered, we would go to the various venues such as the Merchandise Market, the Design Center and art and craft shows to shop for items which would enhance the job or jobs we were working on. We would buy several pieces for each spot and actually place the ones that worked best. That way we had choices to choose from on the spot. The benefit was that we would be buying pieces thinking they could work and those which didn't on the particular job we'd use as stock items for our "Sisters' Shop".

It proved to be a win-win proposition because the customer was pleased to have the whole furnishing event completed at one time, and it made the purchase of merchandise to sell in the store better since we bought the items with a use in mind.

PHOTOS:

"She's washing dishes..." but not yet baby clothes!

There he is, Howard

Me at the speakers' table (photographer unknown)

The "Goody Truck" and us.

Our First Mortgage (FHA)

We had been looking for a house in our price range and came up with one on Riddle Court near Victory Park. It was a small, ranch-style house located on a cul-de-sac that was dry in the summer, when we bought it, but in the rainy season, we discovered that it flooded out in front. I remember phoning my dad when we decided to buy it. He asked how much it cost. When I told him it was $9,500, he said, "The war is just over. Why don't you wait awhile until prices go down?" Fortunately, we didn't listen to him that time.

Donald, pictured here with his older brother, Howard, was born about two years after we moved in and completed our family.

Our next door neighbors were the N e u s t a d t s , survivors of the Hitler era in Germany who, as refugees, had come through Shanghai to Stockton. Ernst Neustadt, the head of the family, who worked in one of our family's furniture store warehouses was a talented cabinet maker.

When the new (Ahavas Aachim) Temple Israel, synagogue was being built on El Dorado Street, it was necessary to build a movable Arc to house the torahs since there was not enough money to construct the actual sanctuary so I,

being on the building committee, designed it, Ernst built it, and Joan Samuels added the finishing touch by embellishing the letters with a translucent acrylic material.

While living on Riddle Court, a potentially lucrative opportunity presented itself. An AZA friend of mine, Art Samuels (Joan's husband), had an uncle who was in the surplus business and had two ice cream trailers, similar to those Pepsi and other concessionaires take to events. They were like rooms, electrified and complete with all the equipment necessary to vend ice cream, cold drinks and such things as hot dogs and coffee.

It seemed like a no-brainer, since the price was right because "we were family" and there were not many vending stations of that sort being used at the time. This was when McDonald's was still a small and local business, and with the right kind of luck and management, we could have been their competition.

We bought one of the units, leased a lot across the street from the community swimming pool in the new upscale subdivision called Lincoln Village, hooked up the electricity and set up shop.

The possibilities seemed limitless, but since I was still working at the family furniture store and Art was in the burlap sack business, we needed people to mind the ice cream business during the day when we were otherwise employed.

We were in luck – a reverend friend of Art's offered to send shifts of women from his church to handle the day-to-day operations. We thought this was a great plan, since they were churchgoing folks and we would not have to worry about the money aspect. What we didn't take into account was that when there were electrical outages in this new subdivision, the ice cream went down the drain, ultimately causing us to abandon that location.

While we were searching for a place to store this behemoth, a new and even more promising opportunity arose: We were offered a spot at the annual San Joaquin County Fair. When signing the papers, however, we were told that all the ice cream spots had been allotted. Undaunted, we began to think of other products we could sell from our booth, and came up with the perfect item: Frozen bananas. This very Fair oriented item was welcomed and we were given a location right next to the midway and told there was yet another spot available for that type of product at the very entrance to the fair.

We were in luck. There was one more of these units available from Art's uncle and at an even more greatly reduced "Family price", an additional stoke of luck which would not only allow us to recoup our losses from the Lincoln Village site, but renew our dreams of making our fortune.

This time, we took our vacations during the fair, and with our wives and a couple of other employees – including Karen Guthertz, the daughter of our friends in San Francisco – we went to work peeling hundreds of bananas, coating them with lemon juice, and then freezing them in preparation for our bonanza.

Fair week proved to be the coldest on record and potential customers walked right past our booths in search of coffee, which we didn't have a license to serve. So much for the dreams we had of instant wealth.

Next came the problem of where to store these "jinx mobiles", as I began calling them. Every day after the fair, we would get calls from the authorities, first asking us to move them out, and then imposing a deadline and threats of a huge penalty. Fortunately, cousin Al Davidson, who always seemed to be available to help a friend or relative in need, moved them to his Acme Truck and Equipment Sales lot and eventually sold them for us.

We licked our wounds in the form of payments to the bank for some time afterward and learned another lesson:

Stick to what you know best.

PHOTOS:

Our home on Riddle Court.
Howard and Donald

On Solano (G.I. Bill)

When Harriet and I got the urge to build our own home in a new subdivision, Colonial Heights, we chose a stock plan, modified it, and hired a general contractor who did everything we asked. He had one shortcoming, however: He was an avid hunter. This

proved exasperating because he disappeared for a week or two whenever a species was in season, leaving others in charge – subcontractors with whom we had no relationship and who at times could not read the plans properly. Several times we had to hold up the work until he came back because I, on going out to the site every day, would find mistakes, which, if left in place, would have lead to a great deal of tearing out and rebuilding as well as much arguing. Seeing as there were no cell phones in those days, it was impossible to reach anyone in the wilds.

We finally moved into the house, which we loved. It had a family room that was special and was in a school district which had a great elementary school for Howard and Donald.

The boys did well in school and were involved in extracurricular activities, as well.

Howard engaged in sports, and when Donald was older, he took to acting and comedy.

We had great neighbors in Colonial Heights, some of whom we still occasionally see.

An interesting anecdote concerning our living in Colonial Heights (about five miles from the center of town), was that Grandma Noonie, being one of the first advocates against sprawl, would not come visit us for many years. When asked why, she explained that she wouldn't go out to "Crazy Village".

She, reluctantly, broke down when we had a special family event at our house and from then on she visited us....even in "Crazy Village".

PHOTO:

Our home on Solano Street in Colonial Heights

The "Gettysburg Address" (Cal Vet)

We had lived on Solano Street for several years and one day, by chance, while shopping in Berg's Clothing Store, I ran into a friend in whose house I had had installed carpet a few years earlier. He told me he had been transferred out of town and, remembering how much I liked his house, asked if I was interested in buying it.

He offered it to us at a price we could afford and, after showing it to Harriet, we sat in his kitchen, drew up all the papers, and that was it. In 1965, when both life and paperwork were simpler, two parties could draw up an agreement without several professionals being involved. We moved to our present home at 6851 Gettysburg Place and have loved it from the start.

Our neighbors, Mary and Richard Rogers, are really special. We respect each other's privacy, yet engage in anything that might benefit or interest one another. Richard and I have attended the Gong luncheons together, and vie to be the first out on Monday morning to bring in the garbage cans. Since our homes face the schoolyard, where much trash accumulates, we use our pickup sticks to ensure the frontage stays neat and clean.

Living across from the Lincoln Village Shopping Center, we have everything we need within walking distance so that while we age we can still see our future here.

Our house also faces the Lincoln Elementary School play yard and, while typing on my computer, I look across at children of all colors and sizes running and jumping all over each other. This not only adds another dimension to my day, but makes me realize that people, children in this case, given equal status in a common space get along just fine.

PHOTO:

Our house which is across from the Lincoln Shopping Center and the Lincoln Elementary School play yard.

Our Progeny

Our older son, Howard Louis Corren, was born on July 30, 1949. We named him after his maternal grandfather, Harry Louis Berman, who died at the young age of thirty-nine.

Howard was a model student at the elementary school in Colonial Heights but didn't start out that way in school. He started his schooling in kindergarten at the Victory School when we were still living on Riddle Court, and every day his teacher, Mrs. Rabb, would send him home with a note attached to his shirt, indicating that he had been sent to the principal's office or made to sit outside the classroom because he was disruptive. Harriet was instructed to send her own note back on his shirt to embarrass him, but nothing seemed to work; however, just before he was to go into the first grade, Mrs. Rabb suggested that we have his eyes examined. We took him to Dr. Brodie who fitted him with glasses, and the first thing he said when he came home was, "There is more than one color in the carpet." Sure enough, the carpet was a definite tweed of many colors, which he hadn't been able to see.

From that time on, Howard was a fine student, going on to be president of the high school student body, participate in football and track, be valedictorian, attend Stanford, graduate from U.C. Berkeley and become an M.D. at U.C.S.F. Medical School. It goes to show how important it is to have teachers who not only teach, but also observe.

While at Stanford, he spent one semester in England before transferring to UC Berkeley, where he did well, capping it off with a semester in Leningrad during the Cold War.

While he was in Russia, two FBI agents interviewed me concerning the reason he was there. I told them that he was just a student studying Russian, but if you've ever been interrogated by the FBI you know just how intimidating it is, especially given the tensions at the time.

Howard met Marty, a fellow American student, while they were in Russia and they married after spending several years discovering what they wanted out of life. They had planned to travel in Europe after their semester in Russia, but upon arriving in Paris, Howard came down with mononucleosis and went to my old friend from World War II, Janine Roubert, who helped him recover.

After seeing that Howard was in good hands, Marty went on her own travels and later became a leader of many study groups in Russia. This caused her to be considered persona non grata. She says it was very scary while waiting to leave as she didn't know what might happen to her while still in Russian territory.

After recuperating from his illness, Howard continued his travels in Europe before going on to Israel. where he stayed on a kibbutz for about a year before returning to America, where he got a job up north in a scrap-iron yard.

During the 1973 war in Israel, Howard returned to his Kibbutz to replace a kibbutznik who was serving in the Army, and, on returning to the States, became a tour guide and bartender in a brewery in Oregon. About this time, although he had earned several scholarships on his own, we thought the hard-earned money we had put toward his education was lost forever.

One day, however, while working in Oregon, he called to tell us that he was planning to go back to school. We asked if he was going to continue his Russian studies and maybe become an FBI agent, but he said he planned to go to medical school.

We were floored. We thought he might be too old or lack the proper undergraduate credits to be accepted, but he said he had already spoken to a counselor at the local junior college and was told that he could make up the shortage in a couple of years. He made the courses up quickly, but was turned down the first year he applied to medical school and was put on a waiting list instead. The second year he was accepted to U.C.S.F and, upon graduation, became a family practice physician.

Howard's lottery number for an internship came up for Denver, Marty's hometown, and the rest is history. He has built a successful family practice in a well-situated office on the grounds of a hospital that recently bought the business end of his practice and is now his employer. This has allowed him to just practice medicine, which included obstetrics, until recently. It is a joy to see the many photos of parents and babies that line the walls of his office, which sports a panoramic view of the Rockies. We feel tremendous pride when we visit Denver and meet patients who sing his praises.

Marty and Howard have been very active in Denver's art scene, where they've amassed a remarkable collection of modern art, living in a home particularly well suited to displaying it. Many of their pieces are by Russian artists who immigrated to the United States,

some of whom Marty met during her years in Russia. She is now a docent at the new Denver Art Museum.

We enjoyed many happy occasions in Denver and elsewhere with Marty's parents, Gil and Verna Lang, both of whom sadly

passed away in 2009. Verna was a very able woman of quiet strength, and a source of endless love and support for her family. Gil was a gentleman in the truest sense of the word, as well as a World War II hero who lost his left arm serving as a Marine officer in the South Pacific. His twin brother, Leonard, was a pilot who became a prisoner of war in Germany.

Gil had a very subtle sense of humor. One day, while we were sitting together on the sofa in Howard and Marty's family room, I was twiddling my thumbs. Gil looked over and remarked in his quiet voice, "I wish I could do that."

Howard and Marty's oldest son, Daniel, received his bachelor's degree from University of Pennsylvania and his law degree at Hastings Law School. He began his professional career at the height of the downturn when there was little in the way of opportunity for a young lawyer.

He married Jen Liu, a kindergarten teacher who got her masters at UC Davis and now works in retail. They celebrated their wedding with a whimsical Dr. Seuss-style ceremony performed by Uncle Donald at the Brown Palace in Denver on 8/8/08, a lucky date for the Chinese (the Beijing Olympics opened the same day at Eight PM). They moved to Stockton where Dan worked in the law office of cousin Craig Corren for a brief period before moving to the Los Angeles area where Jen's family lives and Dan was hired by local Law Firm.

Marty and Howard's youngest, our granddaughter Talia, graduated from the University Of Michigan Theater Department and now lives in New York City. She began working in musical comedy, where, ironically, one of her first professional jobs was a review of the music and lyrics of Irving Berlin, whom Grandma Noonie always claimed was our cousin! She now runs her own company, a nonprofit

philanthropic organization called "The Uprising."

Our younger son, Donald, initially showed a talent for entertaining when, at about seven years old, he assisted his brother in a school talent show. As soon as the spotlight hit him, he was all over the stage, playing the piano which he was already doing by ear, jumping on and off the stage, wise cracking and making me squirm in my seat. The audience, however, was eating it up and the more they clapped and howled, the wilder he got.

From that day on he was, "The Entertainer" and continued to be so at Lincoln High School, where for four years he had the opportunity to explore all aspects of theater as a member of a unique high school drama company under the tutelage of Tom McKenzie. McKenzie was an enlightened educator and drama director who even took his troupe to Reading, England, for further instruction. Donald's cousin Marc was also in the troupe.

Like his older brother, Donald was student body president and graduated with honors. After graduating from Lincoln High School, where he excelled in the performing arts, Donald attended UC Berkeley for a year, living in a defunct fraternity house with Howard. He then was accepted into the theater division of the Juilliard School and spent the next two years there studying acting before venturing into the uncertain world of auditioning.

He's done quite well as an actor, pianist and writer having had leading roles in two Broadway productions: Harvey Fierstein's *Torch Song Trilogy*, and *Souvenir*, opposite Tony Award-winning actress, Judy Kaye.

Donald has also appeared in many episodes of television's *Law and Order*, as well as a segment of the *Martha Stewart Living, TV*, which for two years he wrote and co-directed. He's performed in many venues as a bar pianist, song and dance man, vocalist and a Shakespearean actor. He's won several honors, including two Critics' Awards in Los Angeles and San Francisco for *Torch Song Trilogy*, and a Career Achievement Award from the Stockton Arts Association. He considers the latter award from his hometown and peers in local theater very special.

Donald's life partner is Richard Prouse, who is not only a great addition to our family, but a remarkable artist. Richard is a leading scenic artist whose credits are too numerous to mention except to state that he is much sought after for his work on the Broadway stage.

Donald and Richard own an apartment close to the theaters in Manhattan, as well as a wonderfully remodeled home on beautiful grounds in a small town in the Hudson Valley region of New York where they enjoy their life and their friends.

PHOTOS:

The four of us: Harriet, Donald, Howard and me
Howard and Marty at their wedding
Gil and Verna Lang (Marty's parents)
Harriet and me, our children, and our grandchildren, at Daniel's college graduation
Daniel and Jen at their wedding
Granddaughter, Talia
Talent show that launched Donald
Donald and Richard

Musings With My Sons

I visited Donald one weekend while he was working under a stage name, Cosmo White, at the Goodman Theater in Chicago. He was in the two person play *A Life In The Theatre*, and after the show we went to the Acorn on Oak, a popular piano bar which featured Buddy Charles as resident pianist/entertainer. After we were seated, to my surprise and delight, Buddy introduced Cosmo White and the audience went wild. Cosmo, AKA Donald, was invited to the front and the two of them played and sang a couple of numbers together, whereupon, Buddy announced that they had a special guest in the room and would Cosmo's father, Mr. White, please stand up. I've always regretted not having had the quickness of mind to reply, "Thank you, but I changed my name to Corren."

The next day we went for a long walk and began talking about the "old days" when he was a young boy at home. The longer we talked the more we realized that we both had "issues" and began shouting them out. This proved to be, at least for me (and I think for him) a very special time of understanding.

Note: Although the name Cosmo White, like other odd names adapted by entertainers, became quite popular and a definite boon for him, when he got his first part on Broadway and had to join Equity, he called and told us that he was going to use his real name because in years to come he might not know who he really was.

A few years later Howard called me and relating to my weekend with Donald, asked if we could do the same. He made all the arrangements and we got together in a very picturesque location where he had rented a room in a B&B which even had a private sauna. We had a lovely time together, even going down into "The Cave of the Winds," but nothing as cathartic as my time with Donald. That is, until the last day.

We were sitting in a very cozy spot amongst the red rocks. Then, as we looked over the canyon to Denver in the distance, I posed a question with which I led with my chin, so to speak. I asked Howard what he remembered most about me. Without batting an eye, he told me what he most remembered was that I wasn't there – that when there was a ball game or some other event of importance to him, I was always working.

Well, I swallowed hard and told him the truth – I'd really enjoyed the work I did to support my family and, although I understood what he was telling me, given the same set of circumstances, I would probably do it all over again.

What came out of these weekends, while shocking at the time, helped us better understand one another, and we learned that the only way to alleviate a hurt is to address it head on.

Another time when Harriet, Donald and I were on a ride up in the foothills a very revealing conversation occurred:

In Paris during the war I became familiar with the Citroen automobile, from the super small one with canvas top and side panels to the luxury sedan with its long front hood. (During the war these models ran on charcoal carried in a round container on the side.)

I liked them all, but after the war, in the Sixties, I fell in love with the Citroen, DS model. It was designed by Flaminio Bertoni and was by far the most advanced automobile of the time. It was often referred to as the most beautiful one as well. The lines were the forerunner of what came later in the way of automobile aerodynamics.

Every time I saw one on the road or parked somewhere, I would exclaim to anyone nearby that I wished I could have one. Then one sunny afternoon while on an excursion into the foothills with Harriet and Donald, it all came to a head. I spotted one of those beauties and in my usual off handed but longing voice expressed my desire to own one, whereupon Donald, in an exasperated voice, suggested that since I could now afford it, I should just buy one! I replied, "What? And spoil my dream?"

With that offhanded remark I summed up my feelings regarding desire and fulfillment:

In some cases wanting something is more enjoyable than owning it.

PHOTOS:

Donald and Howard with me photos taken by unknown photographers
US-spec1969 Citroen, DS w/exposed headlights
> *(Wikimedia Commons*
> *Public Domain*
> *Uploaded by PLawrence99cx*
> *Created: November 5, 2005)*

Early Training in Business

When I worked as a teenager at the family's furniture store, M. Corren and Sons, on Saturdays and when school was out, my job consisted of dusting the merchandise and other boring duties. Later, when I was able to help decorate the windows, go out on deliveries and help the drapery man, I was in seventh heaven.

Phil Lenci was a young man hired by Grandpa Mendel to temporarily replace a truck driver who was going on vacation. He came for a week and stayed on for close to 50 years, eventually becoming head of the whole delivery department. During World War ll, Phil joined the Navy and served his "duration and six" before returning to the store, where he was soon promoted to salesman/driver. He proved to be a crackerjack salesman, and quickly learned to apply his innate good taste to interior decorating.

Phil's father was retired and a wonderful cook, so whenever I helped Phil on the truck after school and Saturdays, I would plead with him to take me to his father's house for lunch. Mr. Lenci always had Italian dishes that I thought were extra special, although to him they were just lunch. One day, Mr. Lenci made polenta, with little birds' breasts in the sauce. I asked how he got squabs so small, and he replied that they were robins, sparrows and the like. I blurted out, "Do you eat those?" He answered by raising his arms in an unbelieving gesture, and exclaimed, *"Americani!"* They were delicious, and I never questioned him again.

§

When I became a full-fledged employee, I was sometimes given the job of collecting installment accounts. It was our practice to make collections from installment-account holders on a weekly or monthly basis. The houses of prostitution, which were numerous in Stockton before the crackdown in the early 1960s, were among the customers who had this arrangement, and the youngest member of the firm was usually given the chore of collecting from them. One particular day, I was given that duty, so I climbed into the "Henry J," a store car that was available for that purpose. This small car was built by Kaiser Motors in response to the demand for a small inexpensive car and was named after the company chairman, Henry J. Kaiser, of shipbuilding fame.

My first call that day was to a "house that wasn't a home" in a nearby town. This was a famous bordello owned by a flamboyant older woman. As was the custom for collectors, I went to the back door, which opened into a large kitchen. This was the room where the girls hung out when not otherwise engaged. I gingerly pressed the doorbell, anticipating the arrival of a lovely young thing. Instead I heard a sweet, high voice say, in an inviting lilt, "Just a moment!" I waited nervously, but no one showed up. I rang again, and the same alluring voice bid me to wait. This happened twice more, until finally, tired of waiting, I decided to go into town and see a couple of other customers.

Returning later on my way out of town, I went to the same back door. This time, seeing a person's shadow through a curtained window, I knocked. Sure enough, the lovely young thing whose shadow I had seen opened the door. Regaining my composure, I asked her the obvious question: Why, when I rang the bell several times earlier in the day, did a sweet high voice ask me to wait but no one arrived to open the door? She instructed me to ring the bell again, and to my surprise, the same sweet voice bid me wait. When I looked in the direction from which it came I saw, on a perch, a colorful parrot!

The parrot episode was probably the funniest thing that happened to me while engaged in the collection department, but some of the other experiences I had were very special, as well.

Stockton was a "closed" town in so far as gambling and prostitution were concerned, but that was only on paper, so to speak, because, in reality the town was a swinging place, with "sin" occurring on almost every corner downtown.

Prostitution was a controlled and supervised business with the proper medical supervision and inspection, which actually made it a service to the community since, at the time, our community had a huge number of single men who picked the crops and had no ties to women in the community. Now of course there are none of these houses of prostitution in town... just as there are no more ferry boats to San Francisco, authentic

Basque restaurants, or a "fishing boat outside the door" fish market like the great Busalacci's!

§

My yearly job of decorating Bruno and Lena's restaurant for the Thanksgiving and Christmas holidays was, in the true sense of the season, a joyous one. The restaurant had been in the family for many years. Lena's father was the owner and the original name was Raffanti's. It was a gathering place for many of the old families. It was not unusual to hear a group break into song, often the old favorites, sung by the Chargin brothers.

When I was decorating, I would arrive about 6:30 p.m. after working at the store, and look over all the decorations stored year to year in a garage next door. If some of the pieces looked shabby, Bruno and I would order new items from the catalogue. I worked until 2 a.m. distributing and installing these decorations and had the pleasure to dine in the restaurant with the family every night. My favorites dishes were gnocci and polenta, dishes I could never get at home.

On the very first night I was thus employed, I was busy getting used to the many things I was hired to do when, along about 12:30 a.m., Bruno, who was not only the owner, but a most generous bartender, as well, came over to me and said, "Hey, Duke," – he called everyone Duke – "sit down and have a Coffee Royale."

I was surprised by the invitation and answered, "I can't drink while I'm working," and he replied in his heavy Italian accent, "How you do this work, you no dream?" In the future I just took it as it came and became not just an employee, but a part of the family.

PHOTOS:

Phil Lenci
Photo of Bruno and Lenas
Bruno and Lena's Poster, (Courtesy of Leanne Marraccini)

Tales of the Buyer

I was made an assistant buyer in the lamp department and began to learn from my dad and uncles the art of buying merchandise. It was wonderful to travel with them to the markets and see all the merchandise being offered for the new season. That was especially true when we went into San Francisco and Los Angeles on buying trips. In those days, everything was written on a tablet, and inventory had to be taken by sight and by hand. What a difference a mere 50 years has made in the way merchandise is handled and accounted for. Inventories are now recorded on computers, often from many miles – even continents – away, without anyone ever seeing the merchandise.

I enjoyed the conviviality of the road salesmen (there were very few women in the trade at the time). It was like visiting with old friends, since many of them had been invited to our home for dinner when I was growing up. Often, when I arrived at the showroom of a particularly good friend, he would invite me to lunch and we would spend a pleasant time together. I must add that his expense account made the experience even more pleasant for me. Of course, there is the old adage that there is no free lunch, and so it was. Whenever I was taken to lunch, especially in the early years, I could be expected to buy a few more lamps, which I did – to the dismay of my Uncle Maurice, the comptroller.

This reminds me of a very embarrassing lunchtime faux pas which haunted me for years afterward. I was invited to lunch by Richard (Dick) Miller, a young lamp salesman Harriet had known when she was a girl in San Francisco. We went to the Hotel Stockton, which had a posh restaurant at the time, complete with male waiters.

On the menu was a soup called vichyssoise, which I'd seen on menus but never ordered. Wanting to impress him, I ordered a bowl and spoke of my experiences in France. Then, when the soup arrived, in a small tureen, with a napkin between it and the saucer, I took a spoonful and informed the waiter the soup was cold. That cost me two extra lamps, embarrassment and ribbing for many years.

A fabric salesman who seemed to be a proper Englishman often invited me to a favorite Indian restaurant near his showroom. The decor was right out of Kipling, complete with a doorman clad appropriately in a bright red great coat and tall headdress to match. I wanted to greet him with "Punjab" or some other word I had heard in a movie – possibly "Gunga Din." The aroma of foreign spices was overwhelming.

When handed the huge red cloth-covered menu with pictures of sultans and other figures afoot and on horseback, clad in tight-bottom blossomed pants and wielding sabers, I didn't know one exotic dish from another. I asked my host to order whatever he liked best for me, and so he did. On my first mouthful, however, I gasped, sputtered and reached for the Indian beer that had been ordered earlier. It was the hottest, spiciest morsel of food that had ever tortured my mouth and throat. My neck broke out in a profuse sweat. I left the restaurant posthaste and, although I returned with him other times, I never again let him order for me.

On one trip, I bought more lamps than Uncle Maurice thought I should have, so he telegraphed the representative in San Francisco to cancel the order. The next time I visited the showroom, I was asked about the fire. "What fire?" I asked. He showed me Uncle Maurice's telegram, which read, "Cancel order. Fire out of town." The telegram Uncle Maurice had meant to send? "Cancel order, buyer out of town."

One afternoon, Hillard and I went out to the Delta Islands to make a delivery to a ranch. When we arrived, our customer was grilling steaks for her workers in a small alcove next to the dining room. She invited us to stay and eat, which we did without thinking about calling our new wives. Compounding the problem was that upon departing, we discovered we had a flat tire and no spare. What to do? Our hosts and the farmhands began looking for someone nearby who had the same kind of wheel we had, finally finding one about three miles away. One of the men drove us over to get it and put the tire on for us, after which we headed back to town. When we arrived home, we found that our family – particularly our wives – had been frantic. They were happy to see us in one piece – that is until the joy of our return wore off.

One day, in the carpet department while I was turning back the rugs on the display pile, a customer brought in a beautiful young blonde woman who marveled at everything in the store. Whenever something caught her fancy she would exclaim, "piękny!" which I later discovered was Polish for "beautiful." We later became friends and since then, whenever we meet I remind her of that incident, adding, as I point a finger at her, "piękny!" She smiles, and we enjoy our little inside joke.

There was a row of offices at the back of the store, and each one was designated for use by my dad or one of my uncles. I shared the largest of the offices with my dad and was also given a room just behind the main office on the other side of the store. It became known as the Interior Decorating Department, with racks for fabrics and shelves for catalogues.

As previously noted, I began working at the store about the same time as general furniture stores were beginning to offer free decorating to their customers who would buy the furniture specified. Corren's was on the forefront of that trend.

The store entered various display venues, including the county fair, where we set up room displays that, at the time, we considered to be the cat's meow. Now I look back at those photos and cringe a bit.

The fact is that furniture store interior decorating has become more professional over the years since circa 1950 when Corren's set up their interior decorating department.

Unfortunately, however, the relationship between manufacture and merchant has deteriorated because so many of the family owned factories have become entities of large corporations. There was a time when even a small business like ours could call and speak to a live someone in a factory, but now, with computers making everything so impersonal, that is no longer possible.

The Brothers Interior Furnishings

After working in the family business for over ten years, my brother Hillard and I, feeling that we were doing a good job, continually asked to be included as partners in the business. The answer was always the same, "Who is it for, if not you?" but we were never included. At one point we were told

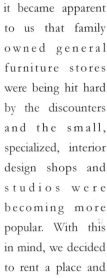

the attorney for the business was planning some arrangement for us and we became quite excited. Unfortunately, he slipped in the shower and cut himself badly. After that he moved to Los Angeles, and nothing more came of his efforts.

Since things weren't working out for us, I visited with a local interior decorator who had a very fashionable shop and a wonderful reputation. He was an older man, and I suggested that I could work with him, with the possibility of eventually taking over the business. He wasn't interested, so I was back to square one. Ironically, when he did retire, Hillard and I were already established in our own store, and he came to us and asked if he could use our wholesale connections to do a little work on the side. We agreed, of course.

Time passed and during this waiting period, it became apparent to us that family owned general furniture stores were being hit hard by the discounters and the small, specialized, interior design shops and studios were becoming more popular. With this in mind, we decided to rent a place and go into our own interior decorating business.

Hillard and I called one final meeting, submitted our resignations, and told our father and uncles of our plan to rent a small store on Central Court from Mr. and Mrs. Fred Stone and open an interior design studio. There followed some discussion as to whether we knew what we were doing and how difficult it might be, but in the end we were wished good luck and told if it didn't work out, we were welcome to come back. This showed the kind of relationship our family had (and still has) with one another. It also echoed earlier days, when our father, Sam, opened his own store, Liberty Furniture.

The next day, we left for the Pacific Alumni Camp at Silver Lake. It was the first time we had ever been unemployed, but nevertheless we took our vacation. We all went, Hillard and Libby, Harriet and me, and our four children, Howard and Donald and Michael and Merritt. We had a wonderful week swimming and fishing (although a certain basketball coach seemed to have fished the lake dry, so to speak). The campfires were the main attraction, leading to loud singing and outlandish storytelling.

When the week was over, we were forced to face the music we had just begun to compose. Our next step was to make an appointment with Mr. and Mrs. Stone to see about renting the store. We spent a delightful evening with them. Mr. Stone was an official in the Church of Latter Day Saints and he and Mrs. Stone showed us the many souvenirs they had acquired while on their missions. We then sat down to the business at hand. Hillard and I explained our business plan and showed them drawings of how we would remodel the building, which was then a duplex with a knitting shop and beauty parlor on the East side. The empty side, which we were planning to rent, was on the West.

They liked our business plan, which was that we would offer my interior decorating services at no charge when the customer bought – from us – the furniture and accessories recommended in the plan. They especially liked what we intended to do to the building to suit our needs. We then nervously signed the lease, but excluded the back half of the space because we thought we couldn't afford it. The rent per month was $150 without it and $50 more with it. Fortunately, we later rented the extra space to use as a warehouse.

We were served refreshments, then took the keys and drove over to the store we'd just rented to take a second look. It being July, there was still some natural light left, and we wanted to see it from the perspective of our newly attained stewardship.

After we turned the key, brushed aside the cobwebs and stepped inside, I broke into a cold sweat and announced, to Hillard's dismay, that we had made a terrible mistake. We would never be able to do all the remodeling I had planned, as the money we had borrowed through the good graces of our friends Harold Berg and Carlyle Sobel (who had put up the collateral for a $6,000 loan for each of us) was just enough to buy some merchandise, advertise a little and maybe keep us in rent for a couple of months. It was surely not enough to make all the changes we had planned so easily on paper.

We spent a sleepless night, and early the next morning we arrived at our new shop, only to find that Mr. Stone had been there for some time – demolishing walls in preparation for the new look.

This wonderful man did all the rough work necessary to get the place ready for the finishing touches and charged us not one penny. Who ever heard of a landlord who came by at least every month, not  to collect the rent – Hillard saw to it that the check was always on time – but to say hello and ask if we needed anything. He even brought us customers, including himself and his family.

There was a fence behind the store that cut off our access to the alley and parking lot.

One day we arrived at work to discover it had been removed by someone other than us. The owner of the adjacent property was furious and quickly replaced it, causing the access to remain closed until his property was sold to our cousin, Jerry Senderov.

Along with Mr. Stone who did so much to bring the shop to life, were others, such as my brother-in-law Ira Berman, who painted the ceilings as his contribution.

Most of the relationships we enjoyed with customers and suppliers were on terms elevated from mere business and into friendships that, although not always personal, were warm and trusting. We rarely wrote a contract or asked for a down payment.

My selling style was based on friendliness. I was my customers' perennial "visitor," often stopping at some clients' home on the way back to the store just to shoot the breeze. Not only did this strengthen our customer relationships, but during almost every one of these visits, I was asked about some furnishing need.

I did the decorating and selling, and Hillard did the office work, making sure our bills were paid and that we stayed in business. The scope of work was varied: decorating rooms, entire homes, offices and other types of business venues. A doctor's office would lead to a doctor's house and vice versa; the same thing happened with other professional and business people as well.

We were extremely fortunate that so many people supported us during our tenure at The Brothers. There are many stories, but a few of them stand out, and, like Mr. Fred Stone, these people gave us a boost just when we needed it most. As I've already said, Carlyle Sobel and Harold Berg helped us financially and put up collateral against a loan for us. Without their generosity, we could not have gotten off the ground. Asking our father for financial help was out of the question, as he was a partner in a competing business and any assistance would have constituted a conflict of interest.

When Harold Berg took us to his banker at the old Crocker Bank on Weber Avenue, the banker not only helped secure our loan but was also helpful in steering us toward new clients.

These friends asked for nothing in return except that we do well, which we did from that first morning when Mr. and Mrs. Leonard Covello called to see if we were open yet. They became our very first customers, giving us money up front so that we would have some capital.

A dentist I had done some work for when still at Corren's called during our first week and asked me to come to his office and see about redecorating it. When I arrived I saw that the furnishings were like new and told him so, but he insisted that I redesign it and quote him a price. When I did so, he told his secretary to draw me a check for $500, a considerable sum in those days. I protested, but he explained that one day he would have to do it over and he wanted us to still be in business! He not only gave me that check (which turned out to be only a fraction of what he later used in his home and future offices) but took me to lunch at his country club, where he introduced me to all the members, informing them that I had just gone into business, and telling them how satisfied he was with what I had done in his home.

Shortly after we opened we did a job in Reno that took three weekends. On the first, I went by train to measure and lay out a plan. The next meeting was in the store, where I showed the customers the plan, photos and fabric samples. On the third weekend, sometime later, when the merchandise we ordered arrived, we loaded everything up, including the wall decor and accessories, and proceeded to deliver and set it all up. It was a dicey undertaking as we delivered it all in our old reconditioned milk truck, which barely made it up and back.

We needed transportation for the business, and our father, having just bought a new car, gave us his old green Cadillac for making calls. We kiddingly bragged to customers that we delivered in a Cadillac. One day, I delivered a fire screen to a customer's house, and I mentioned that we were on the lookout for a used station wagon. She told me her husband had just taken their Buick station wagon down to trade it in for a new one. I immediately called the agency and tracked him down. He had not yet made the deal, and we were able to buy the car for what he would have received in trade. The kicker was that he would not take any money, but opted to take it out in trade. A real boon for cash strapped, us.

Of course we needed a larger truck to move big pieces of furniture so, as usual, we called on our cousin Al Davidson. Al supplied us with the aforementioned old milk truck, which we picked up at his truck facility in San Jose. It barely got over the grade on the way to Stockton, but with tender loving care we were able to get by with it for several

years until we bought a similar but later model from a beauty supply company.

Our suppliers, who did more for us than we for them, are too many to mention by name. Suffice it to say that much of our success was not due to what we sold, but to a greater extent on what and how we were able to buy.

During our first visit to the San Francisco Furniture Market as entrepreneurs, we discovered how difficult it was to open credit accounts with so little capital, but were encouraged when the sales representative for the S. Harris Fabric Company turned in our application, and we received this letter from Mr. Mervin Harris, president of the company:

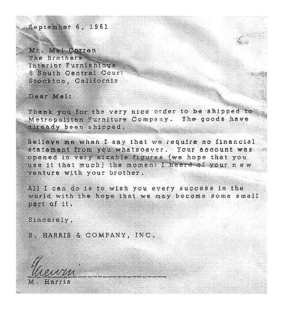

Many of our friends and customers created business opportunities for us. For example, the dentist not only gave us a financial start, but introduced me to all his friends, many of whom then became our customers. The banker with whom we opened our first commercial account not only had us furnish his branch but brought us customers to boot.

A friend of Harriet's put us in touch with her friend who was the coordinator of a huge commercial project. Through him we were able to bid on and ultimately win one of the largest jobs we ever did.

A very good customer whose sister, mother and grandmother were among our first customers went out of his way to find other important clients for us. As I have said, our modus operandi was to collect all the ordered items from the warehouse then load up our small vans with the decorative items so that the whole job could completed and viewed at once. He told the prospective customers he sent us that they shouldn't worry about what they ordered, but what came in those little trucks was another story!

On one occasion, knowing that he told them this, we delivered all the furnishings he had ordered for one of his office buildings and then began to leave. When he saw that we were practically out the door, he asked where the rest of the stuff was. After a little conversation, we went down the street to where we had left the vans and brought the decorative items over.

A newlywed whose whole family were customers invited Hillard and me to lunch one day. When we arrived we found the dining table we had sold her set with her brand new china and silver. There followed a delicious meal.

Her parents were ranchers and her mother fed the farm hands every day at noon, so when I went out there I would arrive around that time. Her father once asked me, as I devoured a large helping of chicken and spaghetti, why I always seemed to arrive at that time. I just smiled the smile of a contented man, and he laughed a knowing laugh.

For a small operation, we did business far and wide, traveling up and down the state to Tracy, Linden, Lodi, Manteca, Aptos, Santa Cruz, San Francisco, Carmel, Modesto, Tahoe, Reno. We even did a home on an airfield in Groveland.

Suffice it to say that in almost all the homes I visited while doing what I did for a living, I was made to feel like one of the family. I watched customers' children grow up and in some cases attended their weddings. Hillard, who stayed in the store and did the everyday business, often remarked that he got the short end of the stick when it came to socializing. I had to remind him that someone had to stay behind and see that the business ran smoothly, because that certainly was not my forte.

We rented from Mr. Stone for several years, and although we never became social friends, we did have a special relationship. Then, one day at the Furniture Market in San Francisco, we were doing business with another good friend, who had been after us to buy the building we were in because he hadn't bought his and now found that he couldn't. We told him that although our business was doing quite well, we couldn't afford to buy the building. In a threatening tone, he replied, "You'd better, because everything is for sale, and if you don't, I will – and I'm a mean landlord!"

The next day, after we returned from market, Mr. Stone came by for his customary visit and we asked him if we could buy the building. He sat down and thought for a minute. Then he revealed that since he and his wife had moved to Oakland (which they had done when the new Mormon Temple was built there), they had been thinking of divesting themselves of some of their Stockton property. So he said OK, and added that we should get our cousin Irving, an attorney, to draw up a bill of sale at a price determined by his real estate man's appraisal. He added that we would just continue paying him the amount of the rent plus a low interest and pay the note off at our own pace. Shortly afterward, Mr. Stone passed away. His funeral was conducted at the then new Mormon Temple in Oakland, and when Hillard and I arrived and signed our names, the women at the reception started to lead us back to the family room, saying that Mrs. Stone had requested that we be brought to her. But about halfway down the long hallway, Mrs. Stone approached us on the arms of two other women. As we met, she put her arms around us and said, "Fred really loved you boys."

I still get goose bumps when I think of that moment.

PHOTOS:

The Brothers and The Sisters in front of the store.

Fred Stone, Our wonderful landlord (Courtesy of his daughter, Marlene)

The old converted milk truck

Letter from Mervin Harris, S. Harris Fabrics.

Down But Not Out

At 3:45 on the morning of June 27th, 1985 my brother and I were called by the Fire Department and told that a fire had broken out in our store and would we come down as soon as possible. When we arrived our hearts sunk as we saw that the East side of the roof was totally engulfed in flame.

We didn't have much time to lament however, since the firemen put us to work at once showing them where everything was so they could save as much as they could for us.

Then, realizing that the building would no longer be habitable, we began thinking of a temporary place to pick up the pieces and continue our business.

It was due to the generosity of a life long friend, Esther Fong, that we were able to rent one of her nearby stores on a month to month basis and at a low rent, for what proved to be a two year hiatus from our original location. So with her help, as well as that of our customers and friends, we persevered.

(This same Esther Fong was the first Asian school teacher hired in Stockton, and was recently honored by having a program in a school named after her. She was advised to aspire toward that end by the esteemed Miss Elizabeth Hamburger.)

This solved our problem of where to set up a temporary location, but what to do with the large shipment of merchandise we had just bought on a recent buying trip to China? It was scheduled to arrive imminently at the Port of Oakland and our temporary location, though quite adequate for our interior decorating service (all we needed were two offices and a small warehouse), lacked a showroom. So we alerted some of our customers and, when the shipment arrived, invited them down for a "First Look."

Many who came to the store and bought some of these pieces, virtually out of the crates, have told us how much fun they had going through the packing materials to choose the pieces they liked best and afterward, owning them.

(Our experience in China was the highlight of our many buying trips, since it was just at the onset of "open trading" and gave us the opportunity to not only buy authentic artifacts but to see and feel the "Old China" just before its recent contemporary remake).

Esther's generosity and the understanding of our customers saw us through the most difficult days of our business experience.

Below is what we sent to the Stockton Record's Letters to the Editor:

Some special people

We were awakened at 3:45 a.m., June 27 by a call from the Stockton Fire Department, informing us that there was a fire at our shop, "The Brothers Interior Furnishings," asking how soon we could get to the store.

I phoned my brother, Hillard, and we droved to the store. When we crossed the Calaveras River bridge, we saw the smoke. When we reached the store, the roof was completely engulfed in flame. At that point, our hearts sank, feeling there was no hope for the place we had called our second home for the past 24 years.

As we approached the front of the store, we were greeted by a firefighter, who asked if we were the owners. He then introduced himself as Jim Kincaid and introduced us to Battalion Chief Richard Berger. Kincaid advised us of the progress of the operation underway, running back and forth from the fire and to us. He asked what was inside the store, and where. He advised that they had covered all of our paper work, accounts, file cabinets, etc., with tarps. Later when we were permitted to enter, we found that they had also protected our family photographs and memorabilia by removing them from the walls and placing them beneath the tarps. They also removed old checkstub books and other similar items from cabinets, placed them in a tarp, and handed them to us.

The firefighters then began to remove the furniture from the store to the sidewalk, very carefully, at great peril to themselves. All this time firefighters were pushing the fire to the center and up through the roof, so as not to involve any of the buildings on either side or in back of our store. When the fire was under control, investigators immediately arrived to commence their work. The teamwork was unsurpassed.

This very professional effort on the part of the group and the personal attention shown us by Kincaid and Berger made us feel as though they were the extension of our own hands — doing what we would like to have done if we could have safely entered the inferno to salvage our belongings and business interests.

In conclusion, we urge you: Please, don't throw away that "Something Special" sign, which we have just abandoned, but place it conspicuously above the door of the Stockton Fire Department.

MEL, HILLARD, HARRIET AND LIBBY CORREN
Stockton

When it came time to rebuild, we hired Tom McElhinnie – a contractor, a good friend and a customer – who not only built us a Class A building but offered suggestions that improved its quality and saved us money, as well. This beautiful new store, which won an award from the Masonry Association, was designed by Ramsey, Derivi and Castellanos, who would become our tenants on the second floor. (When I originally met with Linda and Steve Castellanos to begin planning, I saw they were working in a rather cramped rented space, and suggested they design a second floor on our building to their own specification.)

A fortunate thing happened only days before we moved into our newly rebuilt store. A woman named Clarene Daly walked into our interim store and began talking to Hillard about moving to Stockton and finding an interior decorating position. My office being within earshot I could overhear the conversation and on hearing her decorating philosophy, it sounded as if I myself was speaking. So I went in to join them. We told her we would think it over, but after a day or so, fearful that we might have lost her to another company, we called and hired her.

Clarene and I not only enjoyed working together but, would often relish our "lunch *a la* car."

Clarene joining us at that moment was another of our lucky breaks. Clarene was great and her organizational skills were truly a blessing. We had hopes that she and her husband Jack, an architect, might take over the business when we retired, but they also wanted to retire and travel.

The dedication of those who worked for and with us made it possible for us to do the jobs we undertook.

The following is the invitation we sent to the reopening of our new building event:

PHOTOS:

Photo, newspaper article and letter to the editor courtesy of Record newspaper, Stockton, Ca.

My photo of groundbreaking

The new store

Invitation to the reopening of The Brothers new store.

The **brothers**

are pleased to announce
the opening of their new studio
at its former location
and cordially invite you to an
Open House
on Thursday, October eighth
Nineteen hundred and eighty-seven
four-thirty to seven-thirty
6 South Central Court
Stockton, California

Closing The Brothers

In 1998, we decided to sell the building and retire (we wanted to sell the business as well, but there was no market for a small furniture business at the time). Acting on the suggestion of our real estate agent, we petitioned the city to turn each of our two floors into a separate condominium. It was a brilliant idea, but took a full year to be approved.

Architectural Amenities, a fashionable decorative-plumbing supply company, bought the downstairs portion, and Lesovsky and Donaldson, an architectural firm, bought the upstairs. Our former space was first occupied by Architectural Amenities and later an interior decorating shop, called Ambiance, and at this time is occupied by a dance studio.

When escrow was about to close, Hillard's wife Libby took sick with what they thought was pneumonia, but later was discovered to be an acute attack of a blood disease she had suffered secretly for nearly 12 years. Sadly, she died from a devastating stroke and was not able to enjoy the fruits of our mutual efforts. Hillard celebrated a hollow victory without wife or business. The sadness of her funeral day was twofold, since it was coupled with the unveiling of our mother's gravestone.

During this trying time, Hillard's involvement in the temple was his lifeline. Rabbi Jason Gwasdoff and his wife, Cantorial soloist, Lindy Passer, filled his time and gave him *raison d'etre*.

After Hillard mourned Libby's passing for over a year, he began living a full life again. Around that time there was an interesting development: Florence, "The dazzling red head", had been widowed by her second husband a few years before, and she and Hillard became an item. They have been living in a state of bliss ever since. "What goes around, comes around!"

When we closed and decided to become consultants, as many retirees do, so we sent the following letter to our mailing list:

> *Well, it's been 38 wonderful years, and we can truthfully say, "It's been fun, it's been fulfilling, and as a result, it's been rewarding."*
>
> *All the above because we've tried to offer what our family had: Friendship, Quality and Service.*
>
> *And now, as we change our focus and become what is usually described as a consulting service, we reflect on those wonderful years we've enjoyed here at The Brothers Interior Furnishings and hope that you have enjoyed as much doing business with us as we have with you.*
>
> *Sincerely,*
> *The brothers*
> *Mel and Hillard Corren*
> *P.S. Should you have need for consultation with regard to home furnishings or help in locating and hanging wall decor or decorative items,*

please call on us. Our phone number
will remain the same: (209) 464-7355.

Our focus was on the retirees who had been our customers and were now moving to smaller quarters or to retirement homes such as O'Connor Woods. We would go to their homes, size up what they had, make a plan of the new home or apartment, and help them decide what they could and could not take. At the new location, we would arrange the furniture, hang the wall decor and place the decorative items appropriately.

After doing consulting for about a year, the work, although profitable, became a burden on our free time and we decided to call it quits. But how could we refuse our services to people who had been our customers, many since we began? Then one day an exceptionally good customer called to say they were building another home on a new ranch and asked me to come out and help them furnish it. We tried to make an appointment, but I had so many things lined up that we had trouble nailing down a time. She finally told me if I wanted to say no, just do it.

So I did.

And after having said no to such a good customer, I could not say yes again to anyone else. That officially ended my career as an interior decorator, and I haven't regretted it for a moment.

In former times, when we were traveling and we passed a furniture store, I always wanted to go in and look around for ideas. These days, I no longer have that desire. It was great while it was great, but in our final years we witnessed such a change in the furniture business that it was no longer fun. The conviviality we once enjoyed with the salesmen on the road and the people we knew in the factories no longer existed.

I believe that whatever degree of success I had as an interior decorator was due to my ability to think and plan outside the box. I know that phrase has been used to a tiring degree, but I remember that when confronted with a seemingly impossible problem with an arrangement or room, I would just sit and let my mind wander. Eventually, a solution would emerge.

The Travel Planner

Twice while working with customers, I found myself in the role of a travel advisor. The first instance was when a young couple began working with me to furnish their first home. We had just begun looking at plans and deciding what they would buy first, when the husband offhandedly remarked, "There goes the money for our trip." I looked them both squarely in the eyes and delivered a brief lecture on what I thought about postponing a trip they might enjoy versus buying the furniture I was positioning myself to sell them. I told them they could always buy furniture and decorate their home later, but may never again have the opportunity to enjoy a trip as a couple. A trip that would build memories for just the two of them, before they started their family. They couldn't believe I was talking myself out of a sale – I could hardly believe it myself – but there I was, doing just that.

They did go on their vacation, returned with those memories, and later bought the furniture. This made us all very happy.

The second instance was when I was called to the home of a customer who had been widowed the year before. She told me that she and her sister had been approached by their elderly mother to take a long-anticipated trip back to "the old country," which in this case happened to be Italy. Fate, however, intervened, as it often does. The mother, a "goer" even at nearly 90 years of age, got sick and passed away, leaving the express

desire that the two "girls" use the inheritance from her estate to go on the trip the three of them had planned.

I asked my customer what she and her sister were planning to do now. She said they would still go on the trip, but since it was just the two of them, it could become a little more extensive. This struck a nerve, since Harriet and I had just returned from London and recalling a particularly lovely afternoon, I told her about the luncheon we hosted for a few friends at the Grovesnor Hotel. It had been a wonderful, deluxe experience, although not our usual fare. At that point, she lit up and told me they were definitely interested in staying in hotels such as this and indulging in the kind of experience I had just described.

As we discussed other deluxe methods and modes of first-class travel, she got more and more excited about planning this kind of a trip, and at that point, I must admit I was vicariously involved in the project. So much so that, without hesitation, I lifted the telephone and put my dialing finger to work.

I called the Cunard Line, where I was fortunate to locate a very plugged-in agent who began parrying every suggestion I made with an equally preposterous one of his own. Soon, luxury and money began melding as we created a package that combined the Concorde, the QE2, the Orient Express and hotels like the Grovesnor, the Intercontinental in Paris and the Hassler in Rome.

It was a wonderfully exciting day of planning, and a couple of months later I got a message on my answering machine informing me that she and "Sis" were leaving for their trip that afternoon and thanked me for planning the basics for them.

I didn't know what she meant by "basics" until a few months later, when she called to tell me that they had had a spectacular adventure and that, thanks to me, it was even more luxurious than they had dreamt it could be. It turned out "the basics" had included the royal suite on the QE2, among other upgrades. Could you find anything more basic than that?

We made a date and they entertained me with a litany of interesting, hilarious and moving stories of their trip. It was like listening to two young girls describing and correcting one another during the accounting of their first "away from home" experience.

PHOTOS:

QE2 Ocean Liner from a Cunard ad.
Grosvenor Hotel, London, UK from Hotel ad.
Concorde Supersonic airplane post card (I bought this post card at Heathrow in London.)

Serendipity

As did my parents, Harriet and I have enjoyed traveling, sometimes for business and other times for pleasure. I have already written about several amazing coincidences and lucky occurrences in my life and the following are several other stand outs:

§

We often visit our friends in London and Paris, where we have wonderful reunions, then add on time to take in other exotic destination to round out the trip. On one such trip, we landed in London on Christmas Day and were invited to dinner by our friends Lily and Audrey Morris. They lived some distance out of town and the Tube was shut down for the holiday. The only possible way to get out there was by taxi which was very difficult since there were very few on the street.

We finally did hail one and after riding for a short time in silence, the cab driver became talky and told us he felt lucky to have picked us up, as he was going off duty after dropping us and lived not far from our destination. Since it was such a distance it was referred to in "taxi talk" as a dream fare. The conversation continued, and he asked us where we came from in the States. We told him Stockton, California, and he asked if we knew two auctioneers who lived there.

We told him we knew "Manny and Brocky" noting they were very good friends of

ours. With that, he let out a gasp, exclaiming, "You're going to Aubrey Morris' house? How can I charge you?" He then explained that Aubrey and Lily were not only close friends but also his God Parents.

What were the odds? Overwhelming!

§

Aubrey was a "man for all seasons" and did many important things in his lifetime: He was, along with our friend Brocky, in the Battle of Cable Street when Mosley's march was stopped. He was with the British troops who were evacuated from Dunkirk in WWII. He was among the first to charter airplanes to take groups of people on vacations (notably huge groups to the soccer matches in various countries).

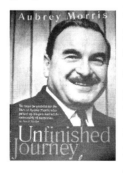 He was also involved in politics as a liberal who, although having himself attained wealth, remained passionate about making life better for those not so fortunate. These along with his many other accomplishments are chronicled in his autobiography, *Unfinished Journey*.

We were invited to a monthly luncheon of his Anjou Club at the Gay Hussar Restaurant in the West end, where a group of like minded friends with similar political outlooks got together regularly. At these luncheons speakers were invited to discuss and debate various happenings in government and society. The day we attended Tony Blair's candidacy for Prime Minister was announced, I believe for the first time.

§

When departing from the Paris airport on one of our trips, we were descending on the escalator when we came face to face with Sam Greenberg from Stockton, who was ascending.

§

On a trip in Spain, we unexpectedly met our cousin Jerry Senderov and his then-girlfriend, who were traveling around Europe in a Volkswagen camper. They used our hotel room to freshen up.

Several years later, after they had married, we chanced upon them again in the airport in San Juan, Puerto Rico.

On a tour of Jordan, Egypt, and Israel, the first fellow travelers we met at the airport were Vahl and Pam Clemensen. The next day, while touring at one of the desert ruins, I dropped a super-small hearing-aid battery. By some miracle, Vahl came over and plucked it out of the sand.

I discovered that he had been raised in Stockton and grown up across the street from my cousin Charlyne, and was a good friend of my cousin Leonard's. He also was an old friend Marlene Belew Hnath from the old neighborhood – the same Marlene Belew Hnath who had been instrumental in reuniting me and Bob Rieders.

§

One time, Irv, Shirley, Harriet and I were dining at a bed-and-breakfast in Aix en Provence, and they told us all about the fabulous junket to Europe they had recently gone on with some friends. On leaving the restaurant, we passed the only other table that was occupied. The couple, recognizing us as Americans, asked where we were from. When we told them Stockton, they asked if we knew the very people about whom we had just been speaking! The man was an attorney from Iowa and knew these folks as former clients.

§

An amazing coincidence occurred just recently on June 26, 2009, when I bought a used two-drawer file cabinet in which to store my publications from World War II. In removing the drawers to make the cabinet light enough to carry home, I noticed a carefully cut out and yellowed newspaper article that had fallen below the drawers. I was astonished to discover it was a clipping reporting the boating accident that killed a cousin of mine on Labor Day, 1975 – 35 years earlier!

§

These three photos show a coincidence I discovered while researching this book – me, my sister, Doralee, and my grandson, Daniel, all photographed in similar trees:

§

As mentioned earlier, the same manicurist who had done Harriet's late father's nails for those many years was doing mine on the very day I was going to marry his daughter.

§

Meeting up with a fellow with whom I'd gone to high school while walking up the gangplank on the ship on which we were going overseas.

§

What were the odds that Irv would come into the billet on Ave. d'Iena at the same moment I called to speak to Bob Rieders on the day I left Paris for Le Havre and home?

§

On a trip to Europe which began on December 14, 2010, we landed in London to be greeted by the worst weather in years. The snow kept coming down but, luckily we had chosen a hotel a block from an Underground station and across the street from a small mall so we got along fine. We visited with our friends and enjoyed the holiday atmosphere.

However, on the morning we planned to leave for Paris the television was filled with travel warnings so dire it was suggested travelers avoid the San Pancras station unless it was an absolute emergency. We, though, being determined travelers, decided to chance it.

We arrived at the station at about 10:30 in the morning where we stood in long lines, dragging our luggage from here to there, only to be shepherded back to the main door and told to join another long line waiting to get on the train. This extended around the block – in the snow!

Exhausted but still determined, we prepared ourselves for the worst, but just as we exited the station, a man dressed in the yellow vest of a Eurostar employee appeared out of nowhere, took our bags in hand, and guided us to the front of the line. Just like that! Not only did he rescue us from that interminable line, he secured our boarding passes for the next train, and in *first class!*

We left the station at 12:30, still wondering at our good fortune, but there was more to come: When we arrived in Paris, J.P. was waiting for us at the exit, even though he had been told our train was delayed by three to three and a half hours. He decided to come early and wait because he had a hunch, he told us, that we might arrive earlier!

Although it snowed continuously in London and Paris, the holiday atmosphere and the warmth of our hosts' hospitality kept our spirits high.

We finished our trip on the Costa Del Sol, in Spain, and celebrated New Year's Eve 2011 at the Apartamentos Bajondillo, where, on January 3rd, the sun rose over the Mediterranean. We've vacationed at this apartment/hotel many times and have enjoyed everything about it. It is very much like a resort in that there are activities if you want to participate, or, if you'd rather sit on the beach just across the road, that's OK too. There's a library, a coffee shop which is also a pub style gathering place, and a lovely formal dining room on the premises.

It's so near the water, it's almost like being on a cruise.

PHOTOS:

Aubrey Morris's book Unfinished Journey
T he Morrises and us
Three kids in trees
Waiting to board the Chunnel train to Paris at San
Celebrating New Years Eve . 2011
Harriet on our balcony at the Bajondillo .
The pool at the Bajondillo .

Giving Begets Receiving

I've been, over the years, involved in several civic and community organizations, and in each case have received at least as much as I've given.

My contributions to Temple Israel have been most rewarding. I served on the board and was involved in two building programs, offering what I could toward the aesthetics of the building. I have also worked on two historical endeavors that brought me a great deal of pleasure. One involved working with the late Leslie Crow, a wonderful historian, who put together the library in the foyer of the newly remodeled temple building.

As part of this remodeling, a landscaped walkway called "Goldie's Garden" was created by Ron and Donna Stein in memory of our mother; Goldie. In addition, Hillard, Doralee and I

commissioned a stained glass panel in memory of our parents. It hangs in the foyer between the beemah railings and menorahs from the old temple which we also renovated. As a further tribute to Mother and Dad, the image of this panel has become the logo for many of the Temple's publications.

I have also been working with Steve Schermerhorn on a project in which we record members of the temple with interesting and unusual histories. I interview, and Steve prepares and uploads the interviews to the internet. These Temple activities, plus the fun times I've spent in the *March 1943 kolot* (choir) and the Purim *shpiels*, have made for some indelible memories.

In the early Sixties I became a member of the Board of Governors of the Stockton Civic Theater, contributing what I could to increasing the attendance, as well as soliciting donors to the annual fund. I enjoyed the conviviality of the board, whose members took part in the plays the organization produced. My son Donald and I performed in *A Thousand Clowns,* playing the roles of a spirited twelve-year-old and his conservative uncle. It was really a thrill.

I had always heard that members of the audience traditionally come backstage to the Green Room (the actors' holding area) to

congratulate the cast. I was so excited on opening night, I went straight there during intermission, and was sorely disappointed to find that no one was there. Finally, it dawned on me that the time for greeting the audience was at the *end* of the performance, a realization that made me grateful no one else happened to be in the room to witness my ill-timed enthusiasm!

Then, after the performance, when I finally met the audience, I received accolades which made me think I was on my way as an actor. Shortly afterward, however, in a future production, a friend of mine acted his part very woodenly. All during the play I wondered how I would greet him in the green room, but after the performance I shook his hand and repeated some of the very same compliments I had received just a few plays earlier. *Lo and behold the face of reality.*

In the early fifties I added "hoofing" to my acting career as "I tripped the light fantastic" with a group of mainly athletes in the Junior Aid Follies at the Officers' Club on Main Street.

In the Seventies, I became a member of the Stockton Symphony Board of Directors, a wonderful group of people who worked as fundraisers and enjoyed a warm and friendly social life. The highlights of my tenure were the annual fund-raising parties held to kick off the new season and instruct new board members in the art of selling the important instruments that kept the organization going. Morris (Brocky) Brockman and I served year after year as instructors, teaching board members the art of selling. We created all sorts of scenarios to illustrate the various methods for selling tickets on the telephone and in person. There were contests for the most tickets sold, the

prizes being tickets to various events and concerts out of town. Along with the Brockmans, we regularly won some of these tickets and enjoyed many wonderful times using them. Getting new members was the goal, the prizes were the incentive. The sheer joy of our accomplishment was the real reward.

The Stockton Symphony Orchestra started out as an amateur group of musicians in the 1920s organized by Manlio Silva, a good friend of Grandpa Mendel's. When I came aboard, the internationally known Kyun-Soo Won was the conductor, who succeeded in raising the orchestra to a professional status. I was still a member when the Board hired Peter Jaffe, who has proven to be not only a marvelous music director, conductor, teacher, celebrity and master of public relations, but a great asset to the arts in the community, as well.

Maestro Jaffe has not only been the leader of the Stockton Symphony, but, along with the University of the Pacific and the Stockton Opera Association has created a larger audience for Opera in the area. Peter's wife, Jane, also contributes by writing the excellent notes which appear in the concert programs.

Several of us formed a singing group. We called ourselves The Whiffenpoofs and met at one another's homes to drink, eat and sing. John McCarthy was the pianist and the rest of us were the troubadours.

I'm not as actively connected nor am I still on the Symphony Board, but currently am involved in planning a Gala to celebrate the ninetieth Anniversary of the Stockton Symphony. When it was a nonprofessional group of classical musicians under the leadership of Manlio Silva, who founded it in 1826, I would often be in the store when the maestro, himself, would come in to solicit funds from Grandpa Mendel.

The Symphony and Civic Theater Boards were very convivial groups of people, which made whatever we did for the organizations a pleasure.

PHOTOS:

"Goldie's Garden"
Stained glass window-memory of Mom and Dad
The cast and crew of "A Thousand Clowns"
1967 (courtesy of Bank of Stockton photo archives)
The Junior Aid Follies, 1950s
Brocky and me, raising money for the Symphony
The Whiffenpoofs

In Retirement

I find plenty to do as a retiree. I am a member of a French club made up of nine Francophiles, plus an occasional guest, who are interested in the language, as well as a wide variety of subjects that we discuss both in French and, when it becomes too difficult, English. We all seem to have a similar outlook on life, and get on quite well.

I always give the same answer when asked what we do at our luncheons: "We speak a little French, a little English, and eat." The founder of this group was Mrs. Bernardico, who, along with other founding members, is now gone. One other such member, Kathe Underwood, who was an inspiration to me and many others, recently passed away at age 99.

I joined the group when Harriet told Marylin Seeley, who worked with her as a docent at the Haggin Museum, that I spoke a little French. Marylin brought me into the group in 1990, and I've enjoyed the weekly meetings ever since.

§

I've been for many years an advocate for the renewal of downtown Stockton, particularly South side of the Channel and the Main Street area. To illustrate my ideas, I created a Keynote (PowerPoint-type) street-scape and show it, with comments, to various local groups and organizations. Linda Derivi, the architect who designed The Brother's new building for us, is very instrumental in this endeavor and I assist her with my presentation.

The photos in my show illustrate what I think should be done, using the assets already in place. I also outline what I believe would be a great transportation system, thereby removing many private automobiles from the streets. I am continually updating the presentation with photos I take when Harriet and I travel to cities that have done similar things.

This is a labor of love for me. I have no ax to grind. I just want to help make the downtown what it used to be – a thriving commercial and gathering place.

Note: For more information concerning Stockton and particularly our downtown, refer to Sylvia Minneck's book: *Never a Burnt Bridge*.

§

I've recently met with retired architect Glen Mortensen, who designed the former Hunter Square Plaza (now the site of the new Courthouse) and the lovely walkway from there to Commerce Street, the site of a monument dedicated to Captain Weber. He is working on gentrifying the Mormon Slough.

His plan is very much like what Denver has done with the Platt River Project, which is not only beautiful but has brought that old part of town back from a state of abandonment.

I was first made aware of the possible-use of old deserted buildings in downtown Stockton when I observed the vision of Foster Fluetsch, who recognized their potential and saw to the rehabilitation of several of them. One example was the creation of "Little Mavericks," a nursery school in a former downtown church, which offered mothers employed by the firm a secure place to leave their preschool children while working. It was a novel, family friendly benefit and if not the first, certainly one of the first ever put into practice.

A similar project, along with an ambitious plan to redevelop several blocks downtown is presently being pursued by Zac Cort of Ten Space, a development firm which is working to redevelop a 15-acre section of the downtown.

Zak is the son of Dan Cort, who not only believes that old buildings can be successfully restored, but has made a career of doing so in Downtown Stockton. On a personal note, Dan's mother was a girlhood friend in San Francisco of Harriet's, and Dan bought his first downtown building from our family.

§

I have also attended, until there were not enough of us, a bimonthly luncheon of a dozen or so veterans from World War II, the Korean and the Vietnam wars. We were of all ranks and enjoyed lively conversations about our wartime exploits, old Stockton (some of us were natives), and politics. Although we were of various stripes – ranging from devout Republicans to ardent Democrats – we always enjoyed the repartee and never tired of our spirited, good-natured discussions.

I began participating in these luncheons when my friend, Dr. Richard Wong., asked me to join him and two friends at Gong's, a Chinese restaurant in town (formerly Gong Lee's, and before that Minnie's).

I will never forget the first day I joined them. I had arrived a few minutes late and they had begun to eat. I noticed they were all eating with forks. "How can you eat Chinese food with forks? Where are the chopsticks?" I asked. Dr. Wong. without missing a beat, called the waitress over and pointing to me, said, "Bring chopsticks for the Chinese guy!"

The luncheon group began with the original members: Fernando Moreno (deceased) and Cruz Portillo (deceased) – and from that nucleus, my neighbor, Richard Rogers, a retired

Lieutenant Colonel who flew helicopters in Vietnam and won the Silver Star; Keith Cornell, who flew 25 bombing missions over Germany at the very beginning of the American involvement in World War II and was awarded the Distinguished Flying Cross twice; Earl Ennis (deceased), who was on the Bataan Death March and spent three-plus years in a Japanese prisoner of war camp; Peter Spanos (deceased) who had been in a German prisoner of war camp; cousin Irving Corren, who, as earlier mentioned, was with the outfit that liberated the first concentration camp, Ohrdruf (it was discovered the same day President Roosevelt died and therefore was not extensively reported); Ken Mar, who was in the ASTP college program and was pressed into active duty before going on to become a dentist; Leo Pochini, a mechanic who repaired P47 fighter planes; my brother the sailor, Hillard; cousin Al Davidson, who trained cadet pilots on the Link Trainer; and Lex Corales, Bob Hong, Jack Hyman, Jim Willett, Lester Novaresse, and Primo Castagno. They stopped asking me to tell my stories because they didn't believe I was even in the Army.

Dick – who was a pharmacist and later an M.D – was a medic during World War II, in the thick of it from Normandy on. He established the Combat Medical Records Section for the 28th Infantry Division. I call him "The General" (Generalisimo), and he calls me "Brigadier". Of course, neither of us were officers – he was a sergeant (even though he was a licensed pharmacist at the time), and I was a T/5 (corporal).

The real General in our group was Doug Taylor, who later lost his son, Mark, an Army Lt. Colonel M.D., who was killed while attempting to save a fellow soldier's life during a bombing in Iraq. Doug never recovered from the loss and died shortly afterward.

If one of the guys complains about a dish that's being served, I remind him that: "We don't come here for the food, but for the conviviality." The lesson is that sometimes what you put in your brain is more important than what you put in your stomach.

§

I had always had a desire to sing with a Karaoke machine, and since I assumed that any entertainment is better than none, I asked Dr. Wong if he would audition me in the recreation room of the convalescent home we often visited. He agreed, so I asked the recreation director if they had a karaoke machine I could use. He said yes, but it didn't work. So I had it fixed, bought a new microphone, a Frank Sinatra karaoke tape which included "New York, New York" and "My Way" and began to practice.

When I thought I could perform credibly, Dr. Wong and I went over for a "dry run".

I had hoped that for the first time the room would be empty, but as I set up the gear, I noticed one woman who I had known for the two or so years I had been visiting there. She was always very friendly and, although she never spoke, every time I chanced on her in the hallway, she would greet me with a cute little twist of her fingers and a very melodious, "WOO, WOO!" So having her in the room gave me the confidence that comes with performing to an audience you think is "with you".

This feeling was short lived, however, for when I opened my mouth to sing "New York, New York," she began pointing and waving her finger at me, screaming frantically, "Who dyah think y'are?" followed by an even louder and more demanding, "Git outahyere!"

Never having heard her utter anything before besides "WOO, WOO!" I was shocked. As she ardently pushed herself out of the room, I finished the song Sinatra made so famous.

I was, of course, somewhat dismayed, but having invested in a microphone and karaoke

tape, I was ready to try again. That is, until I asked Dr. Wong what he thought. He deliberated for a moment, then replied, in a rather low voice, "Maybe next time you should try something a little slower."

§

Our Writers Group is an offshoot of the OLLI at Pacific Autobiographical Writing class taught by Diane Runion. It was so successful that after the final course we students decided to stay together as a self administered workshop. It has become a no holds barred therapy event.

PHOTOS:

The French Club circa 1977
The French Club 2016
Two luncheon gatherings at Gong's, with founder "General" Dick Wong, M.D. (Ret.) with the yellow shirt in the top photo and vest in bottom
Our OLLI Writers Group

Reunions

In 2009 a group of us organized a reunion of the wartime (WWII) classes (1941-1945) of the old and no longer existing Stockton High School. It was a huge success. About 430 former students attended a luncheon at the Stockton Ballroom.

There we all reminisced and were treated to a wonderful talent show performed by our peers. It was announced that any monies collected in excess of the cost of the event would be donated to the Haagin Museum here in Stockton where the WWII Jeep is on display. Willy was bought for the Army by a couple of the classes with the proceeds from their sales of WWII War Bonds.

The Jeep was brought to the entrance of the Ballroom and Todd Ruhstaller, the museum's curator, saw to it that each of the alums could be photographed with the Jeep.

A few of us locals, along with the University of the Pacific, hosted a 60 year reunion of the Army Enlisted Reserve Corps which left on March 16th 1943 from the College of the Pacific. Out of 58 only 13 members attended.

John, Jack, Toomay, the tallest one standing in the top row of the bottom photo was the most successful member. He rose to the rank of Major General and made the service his career. The rest of us, to my knowledge, were of lessor rank and stayed in for just the "Duration and six months" (the required amount of time to remain in the service during WWII).

The University treated us to lunch. We reminded ourselves of the good old days, and the President of the University spoke to us of our valor.

Our family, the Correns, have also had wonderful reunions. Relatives have come from far and near to attend and while eating and drinking is an essential part of the gathering, the most enjoyable part is the "Remember when?" times.

These are the moments when the various generations have the opportunity to glean bits of information that is current as well as that which has and should be passed along. It is a celebration of life which the youngest use as an encyclopedia of the family's accomplishments as well as, in some cases failure...such as buying the wrong stock, betting on the wrong horse or just passing up the opportunity of a lifetime.

These are the events that sum up our *raison d'etre*, and give us the pride in our past and our hopes for the future.

I believe every family – or for that matter, business – needs this time of reckoning in order to focus on its own *raison d'etre*.

...But They Will Be Coming Back

'To Her We Pledge Our Hearts'—
Swan Song Of Fifty-Eight

PHOTOS:

Wartime classes reunion 2009
Presenting check to the Haggin Museum.
The chairpersons of the reunion with Willy.
The E.R.C. off to WWII (Pacific Weekly, March 1943)
The 13 of us Vets at the 60 year reunion
Corren Family reunion 1987

The Inventor

I've always had a penchant for inventing and experimenting. Once when I was very young and my parents left me with a baby sitter, I took apart an alarm clock (they were mechanical in those days). When they returned home the clock was irreparable. The taking apart was easy but I had trouble with the putting back together. Later when I was about 10, one of my experiments caused a fire in our garage.

However, in later years I came up with some ideas which I thought were sure to be my gateway to unbelievable wealth. The ones that held the most promise were:

The "Armeez", shown here being comfortably demonstrated by my wife, is a traveling

arm pad designed to relieve the misery of the hard surface on airline arm rests. I thought it would be a natural for economy flyers until, on one long flight I was able to actually test it. To my dismay, although it proved to be the aid I had imagined, it was a nuisance getting permission from my seat mate before using it.

Then came the "Walk'n'Watch," a treadmill with a TV monitor and DVD attached for simultaneously walking and watching. This seemed a promising prospect... until I went to a local gym and saw an entire roomful of them.

A close relation to the "Walk'n'Watch" was the "Cyber-Cycle", a computer attached to the front end of a recumbent bike. A great idea: recline, ride, and surf. I should have pushed a little harder on that one.

I've already mentioned the Place kicking and ball holder. Those might well have been my greatest scores.

Another great was the "Mazeltoss" on which I worked with Jim Morris. It's a personalized wrapped piece of candy for throwing at Bar and Bat Mitzvahs (The Hebrew means "To Life") Jim and I spent many hours

A MAZEL TOV
לחיים
FROM MAZELTOSS

copyrighting and working on its possibilities but it was short lived. I was later pleasantly surprised when Jim resurrected it as a means of honoring me at my "Stocktonian of the Year" celebration. It was a wonderfully sentimental gesture.

Bravo for My Awards

I couldn't believe it! A friend who I had been trying to interest in establishing a venue for the performing arts downtown invited Harriet and me to lunch. Thinking she had invited us to discuss that subject, I was stunned when she announced that I — along with Ann Hildebrand, Dr. Donald Lamond, Mellisa Esau and John Falls — had been elected to receive the prestigious "Bravo Award" from the Stockton Civic Theater.

I was flabbergasted because I had never ever thought I would be recognized for doing something I had always enjoyed. This award for me was just on the heels of an award my son, Donald, received from The Stockton Arts Council for ongoing achievement in his acting career.

The awards dinner itself was very special, but what made it particularly memorable was how our awards were presented: Each recipient was introduced with a five minute biographical video produced specifically for the event, followed by a specially chosen musical number performed live by members of Stockton Civic Theatre. Only then were we called to the podium to deliver our thank you speeches.

When it came time for my musical performance, the MC searched the room for the performers, but none were there. Following some general consternation, a spotlight hit Donald (sitting next to me), who rose from his seat, made his way to the podium, signaled the pianist, and proceeded to perform his own version of Cole Porter's "You're the Top!" which he'd rewritten in my honor! I was stunned. Apparently it had been planned for months, but kept as a surprise for me. And surprised I was — so much so by Donald's words and performance that I had goose bumps and tears.

It was a hard act to follow but follow it I did, with heartfelt gratitude to all.

I then introduced the members of my family in the audience.

From first to last, it was an evening I'll never forget!

§

In April 2009, I won second prize in a creative writing competition for a short story I'd submitted to the Stockton Arts Commission.

It was a thrill to win this prize. Though not quite the Pulitzer, being recognized for a new skill at the age of eighty-five was encouraging. As a result, I have not only continued to write about my life, but am a member of a writers' group which is an offshoot of the OLLI (Osher Lifelong Learning Institute) classes we have taken from our esteemed writing teacher, Diane Runion.

This class, originally designed to be an hour and a half of reading and critiquing our autobiographical writing, has evolved into first rate therapy sessions. Each of us in turn tells things about our lives which, for the most part, have never before been offered light of day, even in our respective families. You can imagine the camaraderie we have built.

§

In 2011 Hillard, Harriet and I were presented the Hineini award by Temple Israel for our years of service to the Jewish community. Hillard and Harriet both served as President of the Congregation (Harriet, the first woman president).

Hineini in Hebrew, means "I am here." Abraham's reply to G-d's call. This award recognizes the recipient's answering of that call in the congregation.

PHOTOS:

Myself, Ann Hildebrand, Dr. Donald Lamond, Mellisa Esau and John Falls holding our "Bravo" awards

Donald singing "You're The Top!"

Holding my certificate for winning the Short Story Contest

Photo of our Hineini award

Stocktonian of the Year 2015

I awoke early that Wednesday, Dec. 9th, 2016, to the ring of the telephone. It was my good friend Doctor Joe Serra who called to alert Harriet to the upcoming event, although of course she told me otherwise.

I went on to my writing class at Willie's house and took my usual seat. Shortly after we were all seated, Kathy, who had a clear view to the front door raised her arms and screamed, "It's the FBI and they have cameras!".

In a flash (pun intended) they surrounded us, especially me, and with cameras flashing handed me a certificate and a framed photograph indicating that I had been chosen by the Central Valley Association of Realtors and the Greater Stockton Chamber of Commerce to be the Stocktonian of the Year 2015.

The writing class had never before seen me speechless, but I was just that until asked to read a proclamation declaring me The Stocktonian Of The Year. Then it began to sink in and the first thing that came to my mind was, since I've always been aware of my heritage,

Surprise!!

"What would my grandfather, who left Russia in 1901 and arrived in Stockton with two dollars in his pocket, think?

Most of what transpired that morning was like a dream, but I do remember that Tim Ullmer, the recipient of the 2014 honor, whispered in my ear, "Mel, it's your turn".

The actual ceremony was February 3rd, 2016 and when I walked into the Ballroom at the Stockton Golf and Country Club, I was overwhelmed by the number of people who had already gathered.

The whole affair was organized and executed to the last wonderful detail by Bonnie McAtee and Corie Stewart. On the tables were favors – pens with my name and the name of this book inscribed on them, Mazaltoss Mints provided by Jim Morris, (my partner in same), and note papers headed with my name and new title for guests to write the flattering remarks they did about me.

Following the delicious dinner there followed many

Corie Stewart and Bonnie McAtee, the planners and party executors

complimentary speeches and presentations from governmental agencies and other organizations, followed by touching remarks made by my wife, Harriet, both of our sons, Howard and Donald, and my bother, Hillard.

I then, in brief, replied:

"Thank you so much. I couldn't have imagined in my wildest dreams that I would be honored in a way such as this for something I've always felt to be a part of me.

"When I heard the news, I have wanted to thank all those who've helped me along the way.

"First, of course, my thanks to those who nominated me and the Central Valley Association of Realtors and Greater Stockton Chamber of Commerce for adding my name to the list of eminent Stocktonians who have preceded me.

"Mendel Corren, my grandfather, who immigrated to Stockton in 1901 and later created a downtown Stockton legend, M. Corren and Sons, the 'Friendly furniture store'.

"It was he, along with his six sons, including my father, who passed along to me and my brother, Hillard, our love for

Michael Blower of the Central Valley Association of Realtors presenting a copy of the newspaper article to me.

The elegant table settings

Pens inscribed with: Mel Corren Stocktonian 2015 "I've Lived it, Loved it, Life is a Dream"

Stockton and, in particular, its historic downtown.

"My thanks also go out to those who first gave voice to my thoughts for a Downtown Revitalization:

"Michael Fitzgerald who walked the downtown walks with me and wrote positively about them. Lori Gilbert who among others, wrote about my desire for a downtown grocery store. That led Judy Janes, the former head of UOP's OLLI program to allow me to facilitate a class entitled, Revitalizing Downtown Stockton Think Tank. recently morphed, thanks to Cindi Fargo of the Downtown Stockton Alliance, into a dedicated group of people who are working toward a grass roots Downtown Stockton movement.

"Linda Derivi, retired local architect and president of Save Downtown Stockton foundation, my earliest "co-proponent" and my greatest inspiration.

"I'd also like to acknowledge Dan Cort, who bought his first building in Stockton from our family and didn't stop there. Ten Space, Visionary Homes, Trinity Development and other visionaries who are putting their money and efforts into the present reinvigorating of downtown, helping to make my dream a reality.

"There are many, many others to thank including those I've buttonholed whenever possible with my monologues on the virtues of downtown (my wife often noting that their eyes glaze over).

"So now in closing, let me say I hope I can live up to this great honor."

§

Since "a picture is worth a thousand words," I hope the following photographs convey the beauty of this incredible event:

Harriet

Howard

Doug Wilhoit , CEO of The Greater Stockton Chamber of Commerce with his wife, Joan

Donald

Members of my family

Hillard

MEL CORREN

Rabbi Gwasdoff

Linda Derivi

Liz Konold announcing in French

The Temple Kolot (choir)

Kathy Barnhart

Glenn Williams reading my book

Serenaded by Melissa Esau & Josh Landin

PHOTOS:

Permission to use these photos of the event was graciously granted by photographer Tim Ullmer of Ullmer Photography, the Stocktonian of the Year 2014.

We've Come a Long Way!

Ninety-two years is considered a long time in terms of human life, but less than the smallest grain of sand in the greater scheme of things. Yet, in my 92 years, I believe I've been privileged to witness more monumental changes, positive and negative, happening at one time in history.

These changes have not only reshaped geography, labor, agriculture, manufacturing, transportation, communication, human comforts and especially the brutality of warfare, but have had an impact on the health and well being of humankind itself.

Many of these have made for a better life. Others, conceived to solve immediate problems such as the ability to wage war, have brought with them increasingly difficult problems. More profound destruction, the faceless ability to kill, wounds, both physical and psychological which are often inflicted not only on the actual participants but also on those we choose to call "collateral damage."

One day our "Gong Group" listened to the taped interview of one of our members, a highly decorated WWII Air force veteran, after which the member was asked, "How did you feel when you dropped those bombs?" His answer, after a self searching moment was, "You just don't know what's down there.". Those few words evoked a great deal of passionate discussion.

Since that day, I've been made aware that many others who've had the same or like experiences in warfare are beset by similar questions.

The necessity to find enough energy to run the machinery invented during my lifetime has put a strain on our natural resources and created the need to transport fuel to so many distant ports that it's "muddied the waters," so to speak.

Additionally, in order to feed the ever increasing number of people on earth, new insecticides have been concocted, some of which, although developed in good faith, have taken on the job of killing their creators.

And what is to be done about the the many ways which have been developed to proliferate information? They've already created a Genie that scientists are now futilely attempting to return to the lamp. We oldsters were prone to say, "A secret is a secret until divulged by the initial receiver." Today that secret information, due to email and the social media, becomes instant grist for the mill. I cringe at the thought that it may not be long before even our most inner thoughts will be broadcast.

All that aside, I marvel at the sheer happenstance of my having lived so long to observe this era of spectacular innovation and hope it will in the end prove to be all it's cracked up to be.

§

While musing thus, I've put together a list of things I've seen develop over time from their more primitive state to what we now consider "State of the Art":

When I was young, garbage and waste collection were simple, smelly and unsanitary operations. The garbage man, as we knew him, picked up the waste from cans left on the curb and carted it out to the dump. There he and his coworkers spread it out (under the watchful eyes of pigs, dogs, birds and other scavengers) sorted it out for reusable waste, then shoveled it into the excavation which had been dug for that purpose. These days a truck, which is loaded with waste left at the curb the night before, delivers its already compacted load to a designated place and dumped, sorted, and immediately dumped into an excavation which is immediately covered over. The odor of decaying foodstuff, which in the past attracted animals of all kinds to the site, has been nearly eliminated both by the efficiency of the operation and the garbage disposal which grinds and flushes the waste right at the sink. (aside: When we took refuse to the dump the whole area reeked of rotting food, burning garbage and the essence of pigs. When our children came along, we would often return with what the kids termed a "dump dog.")

How many remember ice boxes? Before there were household refrigerators, ice from the "Ice Man" who passed the house on his horse driven wagon, was the way our food was preserved. Later there were sheds that were originally staffed by a live person but were later replaced by a mechanism into which one deposited a coin and waited for the chosen block to exit from the vertical, sliding, canvas backed door. Seems primitive, yes, but better than waiting for the human operator to return from lunch. Today ice is readily available right in our kitchens – from the refrigerator door.

In my "Olden Days", horse and wagon was, although increasingly less, the mode of travel at about eight miles an hour. However, the automobile was in the process of completely taking over at speeds gradually approaching 100 miles an hour. Only a daredevil would dare fly in one of those flying machines. That was still for the birds (pun intended). I took the photo below on the Champs Elysees while in Paris during WWII. It

shows four modes of transportation beginning with the horse and wagon.

The only way dishes could be washed and dried was with a dishrag and towel. Stoves were either fueled by wood or coal and some had gas burners with a "trash burner" on one side. To get hot water, you had to light the water heater and wait, and no one even thought about central heating and air conditioning. (That is until it arrived in movie theaters where moving pictures were in the process of doing away with vaudeville.)

Radio was magic. You could hear music and speech from far off. That is, when atmospheric conditions were just right – when they weren't, you could just hear a high squeal.

And no one even discussed computers because typewriters, pencil and paper were still in vogue.

Life was so simple in those days that children walked to school alone or with friends. There were no police on the school grounds and if a pupil was naughty, he or she could be disciplined by the teacher for minor infractions, and by the principle for major ones..

There were no seat belts, no turning signals, no special car seats or child restraints in cars. Folks would just sit in the car, or on the bed of a truck or pickup and hold on.

Men wore hats, neckties and suspenders and women wore skirts, hats, gloves and silk stockings to just above their knees. In those days a Bikini was an atoll in the Marshal Islands.

Nowadays "It's a boy or it's a girl" is rarely heard in the delivery room. Science has taken away all that wonderful suspense.

The word gay no longer just means happy, it now means happy to be who you are.

Those old enough will remember that World War I was, "The war to end all wars."

And, what ever happened to "A chicken in every pot"?

We've seen a man walk on the moon and drones that can kill as well as deliver packages.

You can watch on a monitor while the surgeon threads one millimeter threads through ours or someone else's body to get to an organ which needs repair.

The social media is a phenomenon with which one can deliver whatever information he or she wants in a nanosecond.

We lived and died with natural commodities in our diets. Today artificial butter, artificial sugar, artificial milk, artificial coffee, and artificial things already artificial are touted as the means for prolonging our lives.

We enjoy watching television and movies on our phones as well as at home on our TV sets and computers. In my day only Dick

Tracy had a wrist watch telephone, now we use them to watch our grandkids eat their mush. Mush?

Having lived into the computer age, I find it takes more time to scroll down to 1924 (my birth year), than it takes to send a text or email around the world.

Speaking of computers, I've had 5 Macs from about the smallest through the ultra moderne one to the present Mac Book Air.

In so far as the economy is concerned, there are many books written with histories of past errors i.e. *A Nation in Turmoil* by Edward Robb Ellis, but shortly after a "fix", repetition begins.

My wife and I were on our way to a social event honoring a late friend of ours, Kathe Underwood, who was, ironically, a Jewish survivor of the Holocaust, when on the car radio there was an interruption. It was a news flash announcing that several venues in Paris had been assaulted by shooters and suicide bombers.

We were shocked and of course our thoughts went immediately to our friends, the descendants of those who befriended me in that city during the last year of World War II. We exchanged emails and discovered that although they were not physically hurt, emotionally they were devastated. The only bright side was that their twenty three year old son who was on his way to the musical event, was reached on his cell phone and called home before he arrived at the Bataclan Theater. They wrote, "The Eiffel tower no longer sparkles" and it reminded me that on May 8th, 1945, I stood on the balcony of the Trocadero and watched as this same tower was relit after many years of darkness during WWII.

In the past we dressed up for important events such as travel, but since the style of dress has changed, due I believe to celebrities and the young's apparent disdain for tailored clothing, the most basic attire is in mode. Denim has replaced flannel and gabardine.

There are probably many other things I could list as "never agains" but to cap it off: In my day the movies couldn't show a man and woman together in bed. They had to appear like room mates: clothed, in twin beds, and kissing with closed lips.

And remember when shades of grey were thought of as possible color schemes to use in a bedroom not what you might do in a bedroom, or for that matter anywhere?

But that was yesterday when Victorian and Puritan attitudes still prevailed.

Today it's no holds barred.

We have visual, musical, poetic, and other means in which sex is brought right into our everyday thinking.

Of course, it was not always the case. In those halcyon days, before the enlightenment of the '60s, our society's conditioned innocence compelled us to keep our delicious inner thoughts in the dark recesses of our conscious and unconscious thinking.

There was not much in the way of sex education in those days. When I became aware of my own sexuality I innocently believed that I was the only one in the world experiencing it. That is until we young'uns got to engaging in a little "Boy's Talk".

I was made further aware of the importance and universality of the sex drive when at 19, I entered the army and was almost immediately checked to see if I had a venereal disease. This was followed by having to view the terrifyingly graphic movies depicting the possible results of actually exercising the desire.

This was followed, unbelievably, by the Army issuing condoms on demand as enthusiastically as cigarettes, both of which could encourage a habit that could be injurious to your health.

But just being a soldier could, by definition, lead to poor health or even death.

Then, a few years later, there arrived on the scene those delicious pornographic magazines, Playboy and Penthouse, which we bought and viewed surreptitiously.

§

My life has been virtually a race through changes!

PHOTOS:

WWII photo taken in Paris,1945
Modern Mac computer

And Finally...

I think the following, taken from a handout I recently read in Temple, is a perfect ending for this accounting of my life and my heritage as I know and remember it:

"To believe is to remember.

The substance of our very being is memory.

We never cease to recite the dream of the prophets.

This continuousness is at the core of history,

and a vital element of Jewish faith ."

Thank You All!

I am grateful to so many people, without whose help, love and support, my dream of writing this book would never have been realized:

My son, Donald, who – after taking me from "I want to record this information so you can write it" to "You can do it. Pop. All you need is a computer" and proceeded to send me my first of five Macs. He also designed and typeset this book while working with me on all phases of development;

My son Howard, who has always encouraged me to write about the family;

Margery Swillinger, who gave me the idea to write when I observed her typing away on the pages of a book she was not destined to finish.

Madelyn Lynch who, on reading the first draft, recognized my love affair with commas, but never the less encouraged me to continue;

Bob Kolber, who not only read and commented on an early version, but returned it encased in a binder;

Diane Runyan who came out of retirement to do the first professional read.

Heidi Swillinger, who read and made corrections;

Sharron Bower, whose remarkable skills as a proofreader helped me appear far more literate than I am;

Catherine Coughlan for her help on this book and also for her help on the OLLI Revitalize Downtown Stockton Think Tank.

Rabbi Jason Gwasdoff who checked my religious facts;

My late teacher, Irving Goleman, who taught me the value of learning from the past and endeavoring to pass something on;

My ancestors, who, in choosing to come to America, made it possible for me to be free and to enjoy the incredible heritage they passed along;

My parents, who by example, taught me how to live up to that legacy.

To Zenographer, Glenn Williams, whose photo of me graces the cover of this book.

I want to thank the members of my OLLI Autobiographical Writing Class for not only critiquing my writing but offering me the opportunity to vent and share.

Also, Jim Nims, a former member of this writing group and a Founding Director of the Osher Lifelong Learning Institute at the University of the Pacific", for his generous citation on the back cover of this book.

Anyone who I've neglected to mention, please accept my apology.

Online Reference

Writing this book was a great learning experience, requiring more research than I had originally anticipated. Much of this was accomplished on the internet, and can be referred to in a "webliography" at www.liveditlovedit.com. There you'll find links to further information on many of the topics covered in these pages, as well as ongoing updates of writings, photos and documents from my scrapbook.

38670742R00111

Made in the USA
San Bernardino, CA
10 September 2016